AN EXPERIMENT IN BIRDING

STACEY PAZAR HUTH and NOAH T. GIBB

AN EXPERIMENT IN BIRDING

STACEY PAZAR HUTH and NOAH T. GIBB

First Edition

Library of Congress Cataloging-in-Publication Data

ISBN: (paperback) 979-8-9947018-0-5

ISBN: (hardcover) 979-8-9947018-2-9

Science & Math > Nature & Ecology > Birdwatching

Cover Photograph, Cave Swallow: Noah T. Gibb

Cover Design & Development: Noah T. Gibb and Stacey Pazar Huth

All photographs by Noah T. Gibb, except where other credit is noted and used with permission from their creators.

Title page: Black-and-white Warbler

Dedicated to those who fly with us,

and to the memory of those who flew before us.

PREFACE

What is possible when two bird-loving people come together, form a team, and apply both their overlapping and unique skills to see the most bird species in Maine in one year?

The short answer:

- The bar is raised and new records are set;
- Communities are strengthened;
- Life lessons are solidified.

This book is written from the perspective of Stacey Pazar Huth and Noah Gibb. They formed a friendship around a common desire to "do birding." What started as an occasional bird walk at the local marsh grew into the concept of 'The Experiment."

In 2025, Stacey and Noah moved from concept to execution by combining top-notch birding expertise with remarkable strategic planning. The outcome resulted in a new state of Maine record of 332 species seen in a calendar year!

Stacey is a scientist. She comes from a 30 year corporate career as a data-driven research and development technical leader in product development. She has a marked history of leading teams with clear communication and pristine planning. Stacey was interested in birds at a young age. After retiring from corporate life, she created an eBird account. With that single action, her birding addiction grew rapidly and exponentially. She became hungry for more sightings, new habitats and enriching connections in the local birding community.

Noah is an avid birder with 20 years of birding experience. He operates his own birding tour business, Noah's Birding Tours, LLC, and leads walks for Maine Audubon. Noah is one of those birders able to hold a conversation while simultaneously being able to identify flyovers. To take an excursion with him at the beach, in the forest, or in the backyard, is an experience to behold. His bird identification skills far surpass the average birder, and he exposes his skill by showing, teaching and doing. He is a quiet spoken man who wants to bird - all the time.

What is possible when two bird-loving people come together, form a team, and apply both their overlapping and unique skills to see the most bird species in Maine in one year?

The longer answer: Read *An Experiment In Birding* to find out!

AUTHOR'S NOTE

The data discussed and presented in this book is drawn from eBird, a Cornell Lab of Ornithology database. There are multiple reasons why the authors selected eBird as a data tool:

- eBird is widely used and accepted by most birders in the U.S.;
- Taxonomical updates are implemented on eBird regularly;
- Taxonomical updates are applied to current and historical eBird entries, thereby leveling the data across users;
- The bird species and *general* trend data are publicly accessible.

eBird data is publicly accessible, however, the details of a birder's annual list, for example, are not accessible to the general public. The authors do not have access to all individual birder data, nor do they claim to know how taxonomical changes may have impacted individual birder data. Therefore, it is important to note that the discussions in this book pertaining to Big Year records and the total number of species seen (either by an individual or in the state of Maine) have been extracted at a specific point in time. The content in this book was generated from eBird data extracted on December 31,

2025. Given that the data evolves over time (historical checklists may be submitted and alter the data, taxonomical changes may impact historical and current data, etc), the authors effectively put a stake in the ground and portray their presentations and discussions as defined by eBird on December 31, 2025. The authors cannot know the impact to individual data pre-taxonomic change. Nor, can the authors know how the data may shift in the future. December 31, 2025 is the slice in time in which this book reflects.

The authors believe that individual annual lists should all change over time with taxonomical updates. This unbiased approach aligns with eBird and reflects real-time thinking. For example, if a bird species is reclassified into two or more species, the species is said to be taxonomically split. If split, eBird adds the new species to all user lists that contain that species. Conversely, lumping is when two or more species are combined taxonomically. If lumped, eBird subtracts the former species from all user lists that contain that species. Individual birders are certainly free to cite their statistics as they desire. However, as authors attempting to discuss data spanning across many years, our approach of using data at a particular point in time (12.31.25) is critical for an unbiased and equitable, apples-to-apples comparison. In no way do our comparisons intend to minimize or misrepresent the great accomplishments of birders over time.

Finally, while the authors have clearly expressed their opinions, they wish to convey that the unbiased data is intended to reflect fact. The data does the talking.

1

THE EXPERIMENT

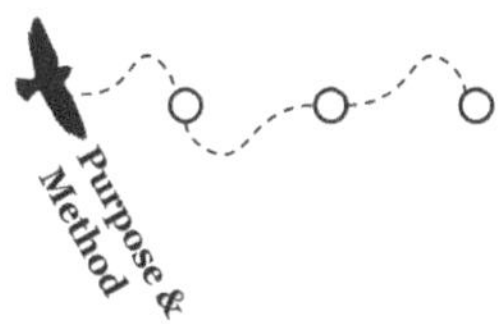

In late 2024, we tossed around an idea for 2025. What if we teamed up and embarked on a birding "Big Year" in Maine? "The Experiment," as we called it, was to demonstrate that our co-team approach and complementary skillsets could raise the bar and efficiently deliver 300 or more species in Maine in a calendar year. From the onset, we believed that each of us as individuals could not accomplish what we, together as a team, could do. We combined birding knowledge with data-driven strategic thinking and came to coining our process as "Integrated Birding."

Birding Expertise + **Strategic Expertise** = **Integrated Birding** → **The Experiment**

With the integrated approach and real-time knowledge of risk and gaps, we felt well armed and excited for the Big Year. We believed the teamwork approach of Integrated Birding created power. In fact, it did have power. On November 7, 2025, we recorded our 323rd species in

Maine, and enjoyed a new state of Maine record. With seven more weeks in the year still to go, we drove hard to stretch the record. By December 31, we had built our annual list to an impressive 332. This was the first time a state of Maine record exceeded 325 species.

A Big Year is a self-imposed challenge to identify and document as many bird species as possible within a calendar year. The region to be birded is defined by the birder. For example, some will stay local and bird in a town or county. Others, will expand to a specific state or even regions of North America, or the world. There are many factors that contribute to choosing the boundaries for a Big Year. Considerations include family commitments, work schedule, ability and desire to travel, ability to allocate and prioritize financial resources over other financial needs. A Big Year, therefore, can be customized to suit the variables in a given year for a given birder lifestyle.

A birding Big Year requires significant effort. There are degrees to the level of commitment. Minimal commitment may lead to fulfilling one's defined goals, and could be enjoyable by anyone anywhere. However, the other end of the spectrum is "extreme birding." When a rare find is reported, extreme birders will drop everything to go the distance. The desire to record a new bird species for the first time, a "lifer," can become an obsession. It is an understatement when we say our Big Year would fall within the extreme birding category.

In 2002, the Cornell Lab of Ornithology launched an online crowdsourcing database called eBird to capture bird observations. It has since become a tool for scientists, researchers, and amateurs. eBird is used to record finds and lifers, hot spot locations, and other relevant information for each birding excursion, whether in a backyard or on a multi-mile hike. This "citizen science" database is available globally and can be useful in assessing the abundance and distribution of bird populations.

Visibility to rare finds is one of many upsides to eBird. Expert reviewers are tasked with oversight of the checklists submitted by users. When a rare bird is flagged, a reviewer assesses the information provided by the submitter. The submitter's description of the bird observed is critical. Photos and/or audio of the bird can be, but is not always, uploaded as part of the checklist. The reviewer then makes a determination and decides if the sighting can be classified as "confirmed." The confirmation process presumably reduces some level of bird identification error in the database. That said, the citizen science nature of eBird is vast, thereby making it a challenge to know exactly how reliable the data may be, a downside. Unfortunately, that downside can deter some birders from using eBird.

eBird also ranks birders. One popular option is to view the top 100, ranked by number of species seen in a given calendar year. The ranking is updated multiple times per day. An important note, there is little to no "policing" of the underlying data that generates the top 100. For example, even if a bird has not been confirmed by reviewers, an eBird user is still allowed to include that bird on their list. The top 100 relies upon the honor system. Here is where "stringers" contribute to the ugly underbelly of eBird. Stringers are those who fabricate or submit false reports of bird sightings. This should not be confused with inadvertent misidentification of a bird - which happens to even the most experienced birders. Stringers typically have a strong desire to boost their life list, and that desire takes hold even when expert birders dispute the finding. Submitting false reports wastes other birders' time, creates unreliable data in the global database and undermines their own credibility. Expert birders are typically able to slice through the stringer behavior and have a good sense of what is a valid report versus what is likely invalid. Misidentification, on the other hand, is understandable, and checklists in this circumstance are usually promptly modified by the submitter once they are informed of the mistake. Unfortunately, the eBird top 100 algorithm does not distinguish between valid and invalid reports. That is where the honor system expects self-policing and integrity. Attaching adequate evidence for a sighting on a checklist demonstrates best practices and promotes self-policing. Even birders who are well known and whose skills are respected may be compelled to provide diagnostic documentation not only for their own credibility, but to give other birders confidence in the legitimacy of the sighting. This is especially true for unusual sightings. The point here is that when we embarked on our Big Year, we had our eyes wide open. We were not going to do the hard work for twelve months, only to have our data questioned in the end. We could not control what other birders reported, but we could control what we reported and how we reported it. We agreed that including photos and/or audio for every new species (including those considered common backyard birds) was imperative to give credibility to our data and maintain the integrity of our final outcome.

By the end of December, 2024, we defined the scope of our 2025 Big Year project. Up to that point, neither of us had broken the 300 species mark in a given year in Maine. To see 300 species was an admirable goal, so that became our mantra, initially.

Noah has been an avid birder for 20 years. His love and knowledge of birds and their habitats sets him up perfectly for an extreme project like a Big Year. He has done the work to earn respect as a birder in the state of Maine. He has a family, a full time job, and Noah's Birding Tours to keep in operation as well. How would the two of us accomplish a lofty mission of finding 300 bird species?

Stacey comes from a 30 year career in life sciences product development - from concept to product launch. To her, a Big Year is just another product that needs development with on-time delivery. With any product development, a plan must be devised, kicked around, communicated, and agreed upon with the team. Our two-person team had to cover a lot of ground and come to a "deal" that would allow our personal lives to exist in parallel with what came to be known as The Experiment.

Clearly stated, the purpose of The Experiment was to demonstrate that our co-team approach and complementary skillsets could raise the bar and efficiently deliver 300 or more species in Maine in a calendar year. But how would we keep ourselves aligned and efficient? How would we maintain focus and deliver? In a typical project, there are requirements that are defined as either must-haves or nice-to-haves. Additionally, the operating limits or boundaries are often laid out to ensure processes are followed and to maintain team alignment. A well-oiled project plan that includes the requirements and methodology can be a rewarding experience that delivers a quality product. Now, we needed to draft *our* project requirements and methodology.

Aside from our requirements and methodology, there are other components to a project plan. Experiments are a sub-component of any science-based project. In an experiment, the purpose, materials, and procedure are the first items documented in a notebook. The actual experimental procedure is then conducted, which includes observations, data analysis, and conclusions.

In this chapter, the project requirements and methodology are laid out to give an overall sense of the scope and approach of our Big Year project. Later, subsequent sections are subtly laid out as a laboratory notebook would be, and include the stories (observations), data and validation, and takeaways of The Experiment.

Following were the must-have requirements of The Experiment:

- Experience joy in the people, places, and birds.
- The "team" had to come first and before our individual bird lists.
- We *both* needed to experience the bird prior to submitting a checklist. This was a non-negotiable team requirement that helped us maintain priority and alignment with each other.
- The Big Year region was defined as the state of Maine.
- Use an integrated process that may enhance the likelihood of observing 300 species or more.
- Use an integrated process that may improve efficiency, thereby allowing more time to spend doing non-birding activities.
- Demonstrate good leadership behavior.

- Observe 300 or more bird species from January 1 through December 31, 2025. The 300 were derived from a subset of species listed in the August, 2024 Maine Bird Records Committee Review List.[1]
- We focused on 300 species considered annual birds in Maine, albeit some are infrequent visitors.
- The 300 species excluded non-annual vagrants to the state of Maine. Vagrants were any species that were not typically annual migrants or breeders in the state. Vagrant species observation was viewed as an opportunity to exceed 300.
- No netted birds that were subsequently banded and released were to be included, unless the bird was observed after resuming its natural behavior. Our philosophy here was that if the bird was not netted, we may not have seen it, especially for tough-to-find species.
- Provide evidence for clean, indisputable documentation. Include photos and/or audio for all new species on our eBird checklists. This choice supported best practices and simultaneously served to raise the bar and lend credibility to our final outcome.
- Use eBird as our tracking tool. This database is widely used and provides unbiased consistency regarding automatic taxonomic updates.
- Submit eBird checklists as soon as practically possible. Demonstrating leadership, as part of our Big Year philosophy, was important. Giving other birders timely information with evidence of photos and/or audio could help the community in their birding missions.
- Our eBird profiles, including bird photos and checklists, were public. Others could both enjoy the project with us and watch where we went and what we observed, and/or use the information for their birding goals. Transparency to our checklists was important to us if we were to, say, end our year in the top 10 eBirder ranking for the state of Maine. If we were not participating in a Big Year, we would have

considered relaxing the public profile self-imposed expectation.

- There were exceptions to the public information. In eBird, it is possible to maintain a public profile, and also "hide"an individual checklist if desired. We decided to hide some eBird checklists from the public in order to protect private residence addresses or a threatened bird species.
- When birding for the sake of birding (ie, no new species for the Big Year), we may not have generated an eBird checklist. In hindsight, that actually happened frequently. Preserving our privacy from being watched every day became essential for going public most other days.
- Day trips were our only mode of operation. Between family obligations, work schedules and personal financial impacts, no overnight stays for multi-day birding exploration were in the plan.

Operating as a two-person team was the most important aspect of The Experiment. With that decision came two sets of eyes and ears in the field, two cameras with which to capture fleeting moments of bird finds. Additionally, and not by design, our cameras could be employed for different scenarios. Noah used a Canon 7d Mark ii with a 300mm lens. His lens yields crisp, professional quality images. The Canon was particularly useful for flight scenarios. Noah frequently would take a picture of the LCD screen on the back of his camera using his phone. These back-of-camera photos would be effortlessly included as documentation on checklists. Stacey used a Nikon P950. This is a bridge camera with big zoom capability. Her camera was the primary tool used for checklist documentation. With the P950, birds sitting in a distant tree or dabbling at the far edge of a lakeshore were a straightforward capture, and immediately downloaded for attachment to eBird checklists. A professional quality image for every new bird would have been amazing, however, the goal was to provide *diagnostic* data for eBird checklists, which was not always a high-quality image. We felt it was better practice to provide "only" a diagnostic image rather than none at all.

As a team, we also had a higher likelihood that one of us could grab a photo while the other recorded audio. Several times, audio recorded by the Merlin application (another Cornell creation) became our primary evidence for eBird checklists. Especially during high pressure chases, our recorded audios would of course pick up our occasional bickering. While the eBird reviewers and public may have had a good laugh listening to our recorded banter, we did our best to edit out all except the target bird calls prior to checklist attachment.

Recall the citizen science nature of eBird? Too frequently eBird checklists indicate "Merlin heard," but then do not include the attached audio. Attaching the audio is one way to raise the bar on one's own eBird checklists, while simultaneously providing evidence to other birders who may want to spend their time going to your checklist hotspot. It is straightforward to attach the audio to the checklist. If Merlin is a frequently used identification tool, consider attaching the audio in support of your list.

Continuing with the team theme, with a team we doubled the ability to do research on what birds to target and where to find them. We were able to expand our critical thinking by having two brains to debate the best options and establish priorities. The collaborative give-and-take was an important factor in our decision to team up. We knew up front that we needed to understand and respect each other's strengths and weaknesses. The outcome of The Experiment would demonstrate if we were successful.

What we did not and could not know up front was how our behavior as birders might impact our level of success. In this case, success was defined as how many bird species we could see in Maine in the year. Would our list of must-haves, mentioned earlier, assist or deter us in meeting or exceeding our goal of 300?

In order to maximize the opportunity for success, we created a plan. The plan was key to keeping us on track and most importantly for taking risk out early. By that, we mean targeting the right species at the right time of year and in the right habitat. If we could gain momentum and rack up species as soon as possible, then later in the year we could be available to chase rarities. This would allow us to take more risk, and be in the far reaches of the state of Maine with less chance that we may have a miss elsewhere in the state. That was the logic of "taking the risk out early." Work super hard in the first nine months, then have the last three months for the long shots. Sounds easy.

The plan, which ultimately defined our strategy and methodology, came together as our Integrated Birding Process by January 1st. First, we listed the 300 bird species we considered annual to Maine. Actually, the list consisted of 302 species. We created a "master" spreadsheet that was subdivided into three "binned" categories.

1. Birds known to breed in Maine;
2. Birds that migrate through Maine (requiring more focus in spring and fall);
3. Possible vagrants (birds not typically seen in Maine; we compiled a short "expected vagrants" list based on historical records)

The binning of birds allowed us to understand the flow and general timing of the effort required across the entire calendar year - and we understood that before the Big Year kicked off on January 1. From there, we identified the earliest possible month we believed each species *could* be observed in Maine. We could have used existing prevalence bar charts from various field guides. However, it did not take long for us to recognize that many existing field guide bar charts were outdated for a number of species. eBird also contains prevalence bar charts for each species. That data is likely "good enough," but our team had expertise that we decided to draw on instead. If it was unclear what month to expect a target bird, then we erred on the early side. For example, if it was possible to observe a bird in April, but maybe March, then we placed the target on our March list. If we were wrong, well then we would catch it in April - no time lost - but taking the risk out early could be a bonus. Our master spreadsheet now listed the 302 species, binned by category, and sorted by the earliest month of prevalence in Maine.

The next spreadsheet consisted of twelve tabs, one for each month. When we both successfully observed a target bird, we would color-code its spreadsheet cell with green fill. This became an easy way to rapidly scan the page by eye and know what species we saw versus what we still needed. Additionally, on each monthly tab we recorded where we went on each birding day in order to catch any habitat gaps in a timely manner. In fact, we had several interactions with birding friends out in the field. One birder mentioned that back when they did their Big Year, a relatively easy target was missed. They were unaware of the miss until late in the season. Another birder mentioned how much time was spent chasing a target bird that they had already seen. With our process, we knew exactly which birds we had and had not seen, and in real time.

We considered our Integrated Birding Process a guide, and not a script. The process was "living" and we agreed to flex with the natural course of bird activity. In a sense, our flexibility was an important factor to taking the risk out early. For example, in May, we may have prioritized a spring migrant over other categories. However, if the opportunity came our way, then we would reprioritize on the fly in order to maximize overall. It was a bonus to see an "October bird" in February, and so on.

Another factor we considered in early January was whether or not to disclose to others that we were doing a Maine Big Year. We already shared our checklists publicly. Was that enough? Ultimately, we decided to inform local birders that we were trying for 300 species. We had a solid strategy, *and* we wanted to gain efficiency by working in parallel paths with other birders. By parallel paths, there were no formal plans or discussions. Instead, if a trusted birder tried unsuccessfully for a target at a location that was a three hour drive away, well that allowed us to deprioritize that target for the time being - which saved us six hours of round trip drive time. That six hours was spent exploring other locations for other target species.

As time passed, our rapid disclosure of interesting species both on checklists (which were generally submitted in the car while going to the next location) and on the Maine rare bird chat group sites began to inadvertently grow our team. Over time, the team expansion phenomenon was plainly visible to us. As we gave back to our birding friends, they increasingly gave back to us by reporting their finds right away. Yes, we were a two-person team when it came to the daily grind, but the birding community grew into our broader team. It grew into a very valuable team.

That covers the primary areas of the The Experiment purpose and methodology.

Now, let the extreme birding begin!

2

THE EXPERIENCE

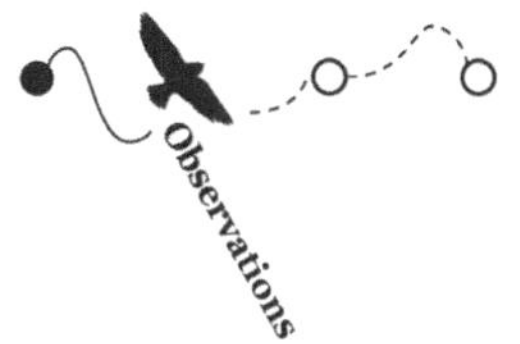

Top: Noah with Dovekie, photo credit S.P.Huth; Bottom: Dovekie

SPUD

January 1st was a seasonably warm, but raw, rainy, and windy day. Not exactly the kind of weather for birding one wants, but nothing was going to keep us inside for day one of our Big Year. Luckily the 40 degree temperatures made it bearable, and besides, bad weather often equals interesting birds. Count us in!

2025 was off to a solid start as we saw some great birds right out of the gate. It cannot be a bad day when you get to see a Snowy Owl, an Eastern Screech Owl, a Lark Sparrow, Barrow's Goldeneyes, and a Snow Goose. Now if your favorite K-pop album goes missing or your local grocery store was out of Takis, the good day could be compromised significantly. Luckily neither of those things happened.

In all seriousness, one family of birds we really hoped to see on this stormy day were those in the family Alcidae, also known as Alcids. Expected species of this family in the state of Maine are Atlantic Puffins, Black Guillemots, Razorbills, Common and Thick-Billed Murres, and the adorable little Dovekie (aka Little Auk in Europe).

Atlantic Puffins are very rarely seen from the mainland, but are an easy bird to see in summer months in Maine through various boat trips and tours out to the islands on which they breed. On those same islands, Black Guillemots, Razorbills, and Common Murres are numerous. However, the real targets in winter from the mainland are Thick-Billed Murres and Dovekies, as they breed well north of our state in the Arctic zone.

All of the above, sans K-pop and Takis, brought us to a fantastic seawatching hotspot in Cape Elizabeth called Dyer Point. This coastal location is a peninsula that offers excellent views of mostly open ocean. Add in the stormy weather churning up the seas and you have the perfect recipe for winter seawatching. Today had Dovekie written all over it!

When we arrived in the parking lot at Dyer Point, we hadn't even stepped out of the car and Stacey called out "Dovekie!" Sure enough, maybe 30 feet from shore, there it was! We knew this was a very important bird to find on day one of a Big Year since bad weather typically is necessary to push these potato-sized seabirds close enough to shore for birders to see them from land.

We jumped out of the car, grabbed our cameras and began taking photos of the gorgeous little creature. It didn't take us long, as we watched the poor Dovekie get tossed around in the tumbling waves, to realize that this bird may be struggling to get away from land. Despite the bird's efforts to swim out of Dyer Cove to deeper waters, it continued to get pushed closer to us.

Unfortunately it is very common for Dovekies to need rescue when they are close to shore. Storms with winds generated from the direction of the ocean do a number on them and oftentimes the reason why they grace our presence is not by their own design. This species is famous for turning up sometimes even miles inland during nor'easters when they should be many miles offshore. When they are separated from the ocean, they will always need rescue and rehabilitation. In this case, the bird could only be rescued if we could reach it.

We had contacted two of our friends, Michael and Bird, who volunteer for Avian Haven (a bird and wildlife rehab center located in Freedom, Maine) to see if they were available in case we could actually catch it. This little Alcid kept fighting and at times looked like it may have been succeeding in its quest to get offshore. At this point, we figured we could seawatch from the oceanside and do what we like to call "doing birding," and then check on our little friend before leaving.

After we cried mercy from seawatching due to the crummy weather, we decided it was time to move on to the next stop. We walked back to the car and scanned the cove for the Dovekie, but there was no sign of it. Maybe our new friend made it back out to sea? Just to make sure, we also scanned the shore and much to our dismay, the Dovekie had now become stranded on the beach.

Now this bird certainly needed to be helped and would need rehabilitation. This is an important note that rehab is absolutely necessary once a Dovekie becomes stranded. They are typically far from 100% by the time they get stranded onshore so simply putting them back in the ocean is not a good long term solution.

Back to the story, we had received a text from Bird indicating that they were available to transport the stranded Dovekie. Luckily we happened to have a soft towel and we placed that neatly in the bottom of a shopping bag. We carefully approached the Dovekie and it was very easy for Noah to pick it up. It was deeply moving to see this tiny Alcid so close. Due to its size and shape, we decided to name it Spud as it literally was the size of a potato. We placed Spud in the shopping bag and brought it back to the warm car to wait for rescue.

After a short time, Bird arrived to take Spud to Avian Haven. We are very thankful that there are wonderful people out there that volunteer their time to help birds and wildlife in need. All we could do now was hope for the best for Spud as it would soon be in good hands.

Now getting back to our Big Year, we moved on to continue our birding for the day. It would be an understatement to say that we were not distracted by thinking about the possible outcomes for Spud, but we remained optimistic.

A short while later, we received some bad news and learned that Spud did not make it. Apparently there had been some head trauma suffered and it did not survive the treatment process at the rehab center. This really put a damper on the rest of the day.

As bummed as we were that our rescue of this little being was not successful, we felt at peace about taking the time away from our Big Year to prioritize trying to save the bird's life. And we felt hopeful about living in a world that has kind and caring people that fight for these birds every single day. All of these factors, combined, equal a big victory even though the outcome for Spud was not what we had hoped for.

R.I.P. Spud. We wish you well in Alcid heaven, where the sea is calm and Copepods and plankton are plentiful.

ONCE IN A LIFETIME

May 22nd resulted in what was certainly the most exciting birding discovery either of us had ever experienced. Typically in May, in Maine, birders are scouring forests, parks, trails, and neighborhoods to look for migrant songbirds. Colorful warblers, tanagers, orioles, vireos, and hummingbirds are usually the stars of the show and for good reason.

The overnight winds, however, were not conducive for bird migration. The weather on this day was raw with fairly strong east winds, so looking for songbirds was likely not the best option. What was the best option? Most definitely seawatching!

Given the tendency for easterly winds to push Atlantic seabirds closer to land, we preferred being on a coastal peninsula. But which coastal peninsula? The answer was quite easy. And it was easy because we already happened to be birding just a stone's throw away from one. And why were we there? A little thing called the Patagonia Picnic Table Effect,[2] that's why.

What is the Patagonia Picnic Table Effect? Simply put, a birder or birders find a rare bird, other birders go to see it and then find another rare bird. Bottom line, the finding of a rare bird can perpetuate the finding of more rare birds due to an abundance of birders looking for birds at a specific location. Fun fact: apparently there is an actual picnic table in Patagonia, Arizona on Rte 82 that this "phenomenon" was named after.

On May 14th at a birding hot spot called Kettle Cove in Cape Elizabeth, Maine, we had some good luck and found a White-eyed Vireo off the boardwalk path. Other birders followed suit and some also saw the vireo. Several days afterwards, one birder found a Sedge Wren in the same location. Continuing the unfolding of the Patagonia Picnic Table Effect here, on May 21 several birders photographed a Pacific Loon very close to shore at the cove. Pacific Loon was certainly a bird we needed for our Big Year but the bird was seen just before sundown so we had to wait until morning.

This brings us right back to May 22 where we started the day walking from Kettle Cove along Crescent Beach and eventually spotted the loon for our 243rd bird for the year! Conveniently, Kettle Cove is right next to Dyer Point which is the same prime seawatching spot where we rescued Spud back on January 1st. With the strong east winds, it only made sense to run over to Dyer to look for seabirds.

It seemed early in the season to see a variety of pelagic species but we expected Northern Gannets and we also hoped for the outside chance of seeing Manx Shearwaters, maybe a jaeger or some Wilson's Storm Petrels, or something unexpected.

We spent a total of 45 minutes at Dyer Point and the seabirding was actually quite slow. It was a raw 47 degrees at the shore. Stacey wanted to move along, but Noah insisted we stay for ten more minutes. Were we too late? Apparently we missed the good stuff? While we did not see any of our target birds, we did have something unexpected. We'd even go a few steps further and say it was unfathomable!

Just over 30 minutes into our less than productive outing while we scanned the chaotic seas with our spotting scopes, Noah said "I have an alcid. It's a large alcid. I think it's a puffin." But it was too big to be an Atlantic Puffin. It had a large orange and yellow bill but it did not have a white chest and belly. Instead it was black all the way up to the head. "I think it's a Tufted Puffin?" Noah said with disbelief. Stacey knew that this was something she needed to see as Noah had also let out a quiet "Ohhhh?" That is Gibb-erish for "You need to see this!"

The bird was initially spotted at the position of about 2 o'clock using the clock system, but was quickly moving north (left) maybe halfway up the horizon. Noah was trying to get Stacey on this bird, "1 o'clock, flying left!" Remember we both need to see the same bird in order to count it in a team Big Year. The pressure was mounting. Stacey was still not on the puffin. "You need to see this bird!" Noah said with more urgency. "12 o'clock!"

"I got it!!!" Stacey said. "I see the bill!! It's a puffin!!" At this point Noah picked up his camera and fired off a few photos as the bird zipped away further north and out of sight. Is it possible we just saw not only *a* Tufted Puffin, but *the* Tufted Puffin? This is a Pacific Ocean breeder that is extremely rare on the Atlantic Ocean with almost all Atlantic records from recent years being off the coast of Maine. In fact, there have been no sightings in the North American Atlantic waters south of Maine. The only accepted records in Maine have been in 2014 and 2022-2024. Likely the only individual of its kind in the Atlantic ocean had returned for 3 years in a row, and now a 4th? And we just saw it en route for its arrival to offshore Maine?! And we saw it from the mainland?! Yes, yes we did!!!

“The” Tufted Puffin

Most Maine birders, including Noah and Stacey, had unsuccessfully chased this bird numerous times in the years 2022-2024 as Tuftee had been island hopping in whack-a-mole style. A classic example of chasing this bird went something like, researchers on Eastern Egg would report Tuftee one day, birders would go out to Eastern Egg the next morning and womp womp waaah. No Tuftee. Then either the stray puffin would be reported in a different, less accessible puffin colony or would go MIA for variable lengths of time before the same vicious cycle would start all over again.

We’d like to add a bit more perspective on how insane our sighting was. From 2014-2024 only about 40 different eBirders had seen this elusive puffin. That may not sound like a small amount on the surface, but well over 90% of the reporters were either researchers stationed on the applicable islands or people from out of state that happened to pick the correct random day to take a boat ride off the coast of Maine.

Want some more perspective? Between the years 2022-2024 which is likely all the same individual bird, Tuftee was reported only on 20 different *days* across 5 different islands. Keep in mind, none of the birds on these islands are viewable from the mainland. Eastern Egg Rock is the only island with puffin colonies in Maine that offers seasonal daily boat trips. The other islands, while attractive to birds, are less accessible. Of the 20 different days when Tuftee was reported, it was only seen on consecutive days 4 times at the same island in this date range with the maximum being 3 consecutive days. Only 1 of the 4 stretches of consecutive days seen was at Eastern Egg and it was just a 2 day stay. Bottom line, this bird was really only chaseable 1 day in this 3 year span! That day, July 10, 2023, was the day where a few local birders actually saw it.

We'd also like to add some more data to help visualize the frustration this bird had created. At Eastern Egg, after its 2 day stay for July 9th and 10th of 2023, it was not seen again until July 15th. If anyone went the next day on July 16, sorry, it was gone. But then it returned the following day on July 17th. Surprise! Time to go back out on July 18th, right? No. It was not seen that day but of course returned on July 19th. It was not seen again that year until the final sighting of 2023 on July 31st at Petit Manan. Given there were no routine boat trips available to birders to Petit Manan, pain and agony was spared that day.

The magnitude of being the only people in the world to see a Tufted Puffin on the Atlantic Ocean from the mainland did not fully sink in at first, but we immediately understood that this was an unbelievable occurrence. Additionally, the fact that both of us saw the bird and snapped photos of it was crucial as others likely would have been skeptical, rightfully so. We both could not believe what had just happened. There was so much adrenaline flowing that even Noah, who never sits down unless he is driving, eating pizza, or driving while eating pizza, had to take a seat on a nearby picnic bench to review photos. While the photos were not good quality, they were indeed diagnostic of a Tufted Puffin. It all just seemed so surreal though, so Noah sent a back-of-camera cell phone photo to two reliable and knowledgeable birding friends, Derek and Alex. Noah messaged, "Think we just had a Tufted Puffin fly by Dyer!!" Both messaged back immediately with one saying "Holy insert expletive!" and the other saying "Holy insert a different expletive!" If that's not confirmation, we don't know what is!

Atlantic Puffin - note white chest/belly vs all dark chest/belly on Tufted Puffin

CAP'N NOAH

A Big Year in a coastal state would not be complete without a few boat trips out on the ocean. Unfortunately, it was kind of a slow year in Maine waters for some of the expected offshore species and this resulted in us having to take many trips out on the water. In fact, we were passengers on a staggering fourteen boat trips in 2025! We can't imagine what that number would have been if we didn't see that Tufted Puffin from mainland Cape Elizabeth. Thank you Tuftee!

We still had to take a few trips out to Eastern Egg Rock. First, because after seeing the Tufted Puffin, we still needed to see its Atlantic breeding cousin, the Atlantic Puffin. Think about that for a minute. It's probably safe to say that we are the only birders on the Atlantic coast to have seen a Tufted Puffin before having seen an Atlantic Puffin in a given year. Wild! Ultimately, we closed the year seeing conservatively 5,000 Atlantic Puffins and just one Tufted Puffin (the one and only) in 2025.

Our second trip out to Eastern Egg on June 6th was very productive and actually ended up being very crucial not only to our success for our Big Year, but also crucial to saving us from taking even more boat trips. We knew it was a good trip, but looking back now, it was very important. Before we exited Boothbay Harbor, we saw a smallish brown gull-like bird loafing in the water. Herring Gulls have all-brown young that we usually do not see until late summer and they are huge. This bird was much smaller. We snapped a few photos and checked the camera LCD screen only to realize that this was a Sooty Shearwater! Usually found way out to sea, this was unexpected in the harbor. Incredibly and surprisingly, this was the only Sooty Shearwater we saw all year.

Once we made it out to Eastern Egg, we had a fantastic view of a Manx Shearwater cruise by just off the right side of the bow. This species is the only one of our shearwaters that breed in the northern hemisphere and it seemed likely that they were breeding on Eastern Egg Rock in 2025 judging by the frequency of reports. This was the only Manx that we had good looks at all year, with only one other brief sighting later on in the season. Our process of taking the risk out early certainly paid off here.

On July 19th, we were passengers on the Downeast Offshore Seabird & Lighthouse Cruise out of Bar Harbor that was part whale watch, part lighthouse cruise, and part birding trip. While we only saw two new birds for the year on this trip, a Whimbrel and a Leach's Storm-Petrel, this trip was worth noting as an experience. Most notable was the infamous Machias Seal Island.

As we approached Machias Seal, it became more and more clear how special this place is. There were Atlantic Puffins, Common Murres, and Razorbills everywhere! There were easily hundreds of these birds in the water around the island, hundreds more flying all around the boat, and hundreds more peppered all over the rocky facade of the island. The birds in the air were particularly of note, as all of these frenzied seabirds were constantly motoring around in circles from all directions, webbed feet dangling behind. It was amazing that none of them flew into each other. Seemed like complete chaos. Imagine if three thousand people each had a wind up toy of a very fast flying seabird and they all wound them up and let them go at the same moment from every possible direction. That was the look and feel of the airspace at Machias Seal in a nutshell.

Of the five islands in Maine that host significant Atlantic Puffin colonies, the numbers at Machias Seal simply dwarf the populations on the other four islands. On top of that, the numbers of Common Murres and Razorbills also far exceed the other colonies in Maine. To put things in perspective, the most one would likely see as a passenger on a boat on the other four islands is a few hundred Atlantic Puffins. On Machias Seal, one will likely see a few thousand. The most Razorbills and Common Murres one will see on some of the other islands is probably not close to one hundred, but hundreds of both species will be seen on Machias Seal. This island is a magical place for sure.

Our pelagic trips during August through September were not very productive for us as far as new "year birds" go. One twelve hour trip in August made both of us seasick very quickly. A few impressive concentrations of seabirds sobered us up for a bit, but we were happy when that one was over. Twelve hours on the ocean with motion sickness is kind of like not having New Haven-style pizza for three weeks. Torture!

Of the fourteen pelagic trips we took during our Big Year, three of them were day trips out to Monhegan Island. Monhegan is probably the top birding hotspot in Maine. With over 320 species recorded there, this migrant trap is about 10 miles from the mainland and is "The" place to be during bird migration. During a Big Year, to be stuck on an island during peak migration could be a risk. It is possible, that while on the island, one may miss a vagrant reported on the mainland. On the other hand, it seems like the probability of seeing something rare in a comparatively small area of land is higher on Monhegan. Plus, if it's a slow birding day on Monhegan, they have a brewery! So it's a win-win.

Our first trip to Monhegan was in May and while we did have two new species that day, none of them were *on* the island. We did have plenty of Ring-necked Pheasants (an introduced species from Asia) on the island, but there are two reasons why we did not count them as a species for our Big Year. Firstly, in 2022, eBird made some changes that categorized Ring-necked Pheasant in Maine as "escapee," rather than "naturalized." Therefore, Ring-necked Pheasants do not count in eBird totals in Maine.

The second and more important reason that we did not opt to count this exotic species is because these birds had an apparent die-off on the island somewhere around 2016-2017. Many birders considered this species countable on Monhegan prior to this time. In the fall of 2018, this species started mysteriously reappearing at first in small numbers and now are strutting all over the island in large groups. Clearly, the likelihood is high that humans brought some of these birds to the island and set them free. We never considered for a moment to count Ring-necked Pheasant as part of our year list, but they are always a treat to see!

Sunday was an important day of the week for us. Noah worked at night Monday through Friday. This meant that Sunday was the only day where he could realistically get up as early as possible for longer trips and not have to work the same day. At the beginning of the year, Stacey saved a fortune from a fortune cookie. Of the two lines written on the fortune, the top line was missing. All the fortune read was "come true this Sunday." She taped this fortune to the control panel area of her car and she pointed to it just about every Sunday in hopes that we would see a bird we wanted to see or would find something unexpected. Sometimes it worked, sometimes it did not.

Well it just so happens that our second trip to Monhegan on September 28th, was on a Sunday. At least three weeks prior, we had penciled in this date to do birding on the island. One problem at that time of year is that the ferries run less frequently. The earliest we could touch down on Monhegan via ferry would have been about 11:00am. This would not have been ideal since we had to pull this off as a day trip. Luckily, Stacey had a brilliant idea.

Stacey's long time friend and colleague, Mark, has a boat and lives in a convenient area to travel to Monhegan Island. She contacted Mark weeks in advance and he was graciously willing to meet us at Port Clyde Harbor at 6:30am. This would mean by approximately 7:30am, we would be doing birding. Bird reports from the island on the previous day of our trip were Western Kingbird, Yellow-throated Warbler, and Bell's Vireo. While the kingbird and warbler are annual vagrants to Maine, the vireo was only Maine's fifth and neither of us had seen that species. We were crossing our fingers wicked haahd (hard, pronounced like a New Englander) that the vireo, in particular, would stick around until Sunday.

Mark met us promptly at 6:30am and it was time to shove off. Most of us are used to taking larger commercial boats out on the water so the mere two foot seas that day would barely be noticed. Mark's boat was much smaller, however, so those two foot seas felt maybe two to three times larger. We really had to hang on, otherwise we'd be banking on our childhood swimming lessons. The adventure had begun!

Shortly into the trip, the anchor had fallen off the bow. While Mark climbed up to the front of the boat to fix it, he turned the controls over to Noah. This was when Cap'n Noah was born! After expertly piloting us for a whole two minutes, Cap'n Noah turned the helm back over to Mark. Noah did not let this go to his head, but made sure to correct anyone that day who did not refer to him as Cap'n Noah.

Maybe twenty minutes or so before we arrived, our friend Derek messaged us that he had relocated the Bell's Vireo that was found the day before. This was great news! At about 7:40am, we were pulling up to the dock. Derek messaged again that he just found a Black-throated Gray Warbler with his tour group. Wow!! Another bird that neither of us had seen before and was a sixth state record. We needed to start doing birding ASAP!

If we were on a ferry that frequents this island, the boat would be able to line up at the dock and use the ramp to offload. With the tide being low and being in a small boat, we were at least ten feet below the surface of the dock and we could not really attach the boat to anything that would keep it in place. This made for an interesting and challenging way to disembark. Cap'n Mark ultimately had to line us up with the slippery metal ladder on the side of the dock and we "just" had to grab it while the boat was still moving. Then we had to climb straight up the ten feet with backpacks, cameras, and binoculars. It was terrifying, but we had three choices. Climb up the ladder and do birding, stay in the boat and go back home, or fall into the ocean. Door number one, please.

Now on the island, we quickly made our way towards the Trailing Yew inn, near where Derek had the Black-throated Gray Warbler. We were both breathing heavy as we did not want to waste any time on this mainly uphill hike. We learned that the bird had just flown up the hill and that it was with a mixed flock of migrants, so off we went!

We carefully searched as we made our way to the area of Hill Studio and what is called "The Chat Causeway." This was where the Bell's Vireo was seen on both days. We looked around that area for a few minutes but had no sign of the rare-for-Maine vireo. Then we started hearing the chips of the Yellow-rumped Warblers. Mixed flock incoming?

We followed the chips and joined the growing crowd of birders not much more than one hundred feet from the thickets in front of Hill Studio. Almost all of the Yellow-rumped Warblers were filtering through the trees with a few other species mixed in, but there was no sign of the Black-throated Gray. Then, our friend Bill walked up to us and told us he just had the vireo. Friends Ethan and Ingrid with their adorable dog Biscuit joined us on the search. In relatively quick fashion, we spotted the Bell's Vireo low in the vegetation directly in front of the studio. We all tried desperately to snap a photo. The bird was just not quite out from the thicket enough to expose itself for a clear shot. We were so focused on getting a photo of this Big Year bird #305 (and lifer for both) that we hadn't yet given each other our standard high five. Before we could even process that, Bill's voice could be heard in the distance, "Noah!" We knew what that meant!

Following Bill's voice led us back to the mixed flock. Bill and other birders were on the Black-throated Gray Warbler and quickly got us on it! We managed to snap a few photos and took in the subtle, but striking beauty of this bird. And then it was gone. A second lifebird! Two lifers for us in a two minute span and just a mere 100 feet apart. Mindblowing! Only on Monhegan.

After losing track of the warbler (and #306 for us for the year), we high-fived twice, once for each new species, and tried to test our luck on photographing the vireo again. This time we had amazing views and actually were able to enjoy the bird thoroughly. Extremely satisfying.

We could not have picked a better day to visit Monhegan. There was no other day in 2025 where there was a species discovered on the island that would have been a lifer for both of us, let alone two! The Bell's Vireo was not seen in the afternoon or ever again in 2025 on Monhegan. The Black-throated Gray Warbler was not seen again that day, but was spotted a few times in the following days by only a small number of birders. If Cap'n Mark wasn't able to bring us to the island early, we would have been too late to see either of them. We firmly believe that our planning (alright, Stacey's planning), hard work, and execution was the key to our success in 2025. That said, we have to admit, there was an element of "come true this Sunday" on September 28th. We still don't know what the complete fortune read or what it was supposed to mean, but we think on that incredible Sunday on Monhegan Island, that it did indeed come true.

T: Bell's Vireo; B: Northern Fulmar; Next Pages: Common Tern, Spruce Grouse

NEMESIS BIRDS

Some birds come easy, some birds do not. The latter was apparent right from the beginning of the year. Not to say we were not successful from the beginning, we were. We had 100 species in January which was a great start, but there was one bird that kept eluding us. It was the second largest gull in the world, the Glaucous Gull.

If it's so big, how were we having such a hard time finding it, you might ask? It's because only small numbers of these arctic breeding gulls come south to Maine in the winter. Iceland Gull is another arctic breeding gull. Typically we see more Iceland Gulls than Glaucous, and some winters, they are both fairly hard to find.

In addition, factors like climate change, food scarcity, and elevated mercury levels in arctic waters have all contributed to a decline in Glaucous Gull populations. Milder winters likely do not push as many of these birds down from the north, but anyway you slice it, some winters are just better than others for finding this species and we cannot always know why.

The "first winter" of 2025 was particularly unproductive for Glaucous Gulls in Maine. In January-March, only 6 different sightings were reported to eBird in southern Maine. Only 2 of those provided a confirmatory photo. Several birds reported to eBird included photos and were identified as Glaucous. Unfortunately, the photos were images of Iceland Gulls. There was another post that reported Glaucous in this time frame but had no photographic documentation. The misidentification and lack of photos was a frustrating theme with reports of this bird as it can be easy to misidentify Glaucous Gulls, especially if only seen in flight or from a distance. Unfortunately, eBird does not flag this gull in expected months (i.e. Jan-Mar) in Maine. Therefore, eBird users are not typically providing photos and are also not providing comments in the comments box. A description would at least help birders discern their confidence level of the sighting and facilitate in deciding if they want to take the time to try and find the bird.

Now, we would like to mention that bird misidentification is all part of learning, and it happens to all of us. Any birder that is trying to improve their birding skills will certainly misidentify less and less frequently over time with experience and study. It's okay to be wrong. Providing photos when possible will not only help others interested in "your" bird, but will also help the reporter learn from their mistake if they indeed made one. Perhaps best of all, sometimes photos posted of a bird reported as a common bird ends up being something super rare. We applaud all birders who provide photos of their birds on checklists and group chats, whether they are identified correctly or not. The value they provide is equal.

We spent an estimated 40-50 hours looking for Glaucous Gull in January-March. And we were proactive in doing so, meaning we were not waiting for others to report. We mostly focused on the Portland waterfront area and across the Fore River to Mill Creek in South Portland. While we saw a lot of gulls, Glaucous (or, Glaucoma Gulls, as autocorrect would indicate) was not one. No reports came from others either until late February and they were almost all from the same spots we had been focusing on. Every time we went back to find the elusive Glaucous, we would come up empty. We wonder how much money that we spent on snacks and coffee waiting for that darn bird to show? Scratch that, we don't want to know. As a matter of fact, this bird once saved us money! We had just left the Mill Creek area with another Glaucous-less experience to go eat lunch at our favorite Portland restaurant when an alert came through on our phones. Someone just reported a Glaucous at Mill Creek! Must have showed up right after we left? We had just sat down and started to look at the menu and decided that we needed to leave and go back to Mill Creek right away. We went back and lo and behold, no Glaucous. Instead, we did find an Iceland Gull, and now unfortunately there was no time to eat lunch. While no garlic green beans and no Glaucous Gull was extremely disappointing, at least we still had that money our lunch would have cost us. Did we end up spending the saved money on more snacks and coffee looking for Glaucous in the month of March? Definitely, yes, and still no Glaucous Gull. Hopefully November or December would play out differently.

Shortly before "second winter," when we were ready to start looking for gulls again, a report with a photo came through on November 12th at the Portland waterfront. We spent the next three days checking the usual hot spots in the area. Meanwhile, another birder reported and photographed the Glaucous. But we came up empty again and again. We went back out on November 17th and were having deja vu all over again, but then an eBird report with photos attached came through. A Glaucous Gull was 2 minutes away at a fast-food parking lot! We drove over right away and there it was. Glaucous Gull!!! Big Year bird #326, and nemesis bird! Finally!!

Glaucous Gull

Another bird that did not come easy, but for different reasons, was the Spruce Grouse. Spruce Grouse are boreal forest dwellers that can only be found in spruce dominant forests garnished with moss covered floors. These habitats in Maine are declining. True boreal forests in the Pine Tree State that are in closest proximity to the greater Portland area are about 2 hours away. Most of these areas are actually 3-5 hours away, however. Throw in that Spruce Grouse are declining, live in very dense forests, are very well camouflaged, can be found on the ground or perched high in a tree, often are found at mountain summits demanding challenging hikes, and you have one challenging bird.

Luckily, most of our trips that had Spruce Grouse on our target list were combined with other targets. So it wasn't like we were driving 4 hours just for Spruce Grouse, not seeing any, and driving home. At least not at first.

Another plus to these trips was that we got to see some beautiful locations that further strengthened our appreciation for the lovely state of Maine. As much as we love the Baxter State Park area and the Great North Woods, the bumpy roads and time it took us to get around these places was kind of a spoiler. The more we explored the state in search of the boreal, we found that the coastal forests and locales in Hancock and Washington counties were our favorites. From Schoodic Point to Lubec, we were willing to return to these areas as much as needed. It also helped that the roads were in decent to excellent condition.

One key ingredient to a successful Big Year is obsession. We spent upwards of 80 hours looking for Sprucey from late May-September. If it wasn't apparent already, it became very clear that we were indeed obsessed on July 27th. After leaving Yarmouth at 2am to arrive in Lubec at 6:30am, we searched for Spruce Grouse for 4 hours. We would have searched longer, but a report came in from Wells which is located in the far south of our state. The report was of an American Avocet, an annual visitor. We decided to bail on the search for Sprucey to make the 5 hour trek back south to Wells. We arrived at 3:30pm just in time for rain, made the long walk down to the marsh at Laudholm Farm, and then saw and photographed the Avocet. Another failure on the grouse, but an Avocet was a nice consolation.

A few more trips with Spruce Grouse on the itinerary were to be had in August and September. Quite frankly, after those trips, we had given up on this bird. How did we keep missing the multiple family groups of Spruce Grouse that people had been seeing? It didn't seem fair with all the time and work we had been putting in. Apparently, it just wasn't meant to be and we had to accept that. We could still reach our goals without this one. But it was disappointing.

Then we were told by a good friend about a spot where they had just seen some grouse. At first we did not plan on going because every place we had searched beforehand had at least one sighting at some point. Going to a location that had a prior sighting did not necessarily guarantee that we were going to happen upon the same bird or birds. After much coercion by Stacey, we decided to give Sprucey one more shot. It certainly helped that this trip would bring us back to our favorite part of the state. On September 21st, we met at 4:15am, and off we went.

The habitat was perfect and extensive, and we searched carefully on an incredibly scenic hike. We had passed the area that we were hoping the grouse would be and made it all the way to the coastline on a 1.5 mile trail. No grouse.

We enjoyed the breathtaking ocean view for a bit and maybe this amazing view and lack of noise pollution was what we needed to clear our heads. All we could hear was the rippling water rushing in and out of the rocks in front of us. This was exactly what we needed to help keep us centered, focused, and recharged for the hike back. We had a choice though, take a new and longer trail back, or the same one we had just hiked. After some discussion, we opted to backtrack.

On our hike back, we tried to look at every inch of the forest. After about a quarter of a mile, Stacey calmly said, "Spruce Grouse." Noah was about 10 feet in front of her and turned, confused. When it comes to seeing a noteworthy bird, Stacey typically reacts as though she just got called to "Come on down!" as if she were on a TV game show - not at all like the chill demeanor of Matthew McConaughey driving his Lincoln. How was she so cool and collected if she actually just saw this bird that we have spent 80 hours looking for? No one could answer this question, but Noah watched as Stacey slowly raised her camera up towards a mossy rock at the base of a spruce tree not 10 feet from her. The tree was on higher ground than the trail, so the base of this tree was at eye level. Noah backtracked slightly towards Stacey and looked back at the moss covered rock and there was a female Spruce Grouse standing completely still on the rock, at eye level, and less than 10 feet away. It was strikingly beautiful and we both had initially walked right past it. It was as though someone tapped Stacey on the shoulder to stop, turn around, and look back. The grouse would have been behind the tree from the direction we were walking so only could be seen by looking back after passing it. How many had we missed on our other trips? We could have easily missed this one. Wow!

We enjoyed Sprucey and spent a solid 20 minutes photographing this amazing bird. During that time, we realized that there was another grouse right next to Sprucey! Sprucey 1 and Sprucey 2! After photographing both birds, they eventually started waddling towards us through the understory and passed Stacey just a few feet away. They picked at some foliage at the edge of the trail briefly, then crossed the trail and vanished into the woods. Immediately after, a smattering of about 15-20 hikers started walking past us. This was after not seeing a soul on the entire hike. What timing! We finally did it after all this time and effort. While it was bird number 303 for the year, it was more than a number. It was an experience and was a well earned gift.

Spruce Grouse

THE FRUITS OF OUR LABOR

The best moments in birdwatching can come from a variety of circumstances. Finding a flock of Cedar Waxwings dangling from clusters of red berries against a snowy backdrop can brighten any day. Experiencing the excitement of a new birder getting their first ever look at the blaze orange throat of a Blackburnian Warbler can bring overwhelming joy. Hearing a sudden splash and watching an Osprey fly off with a fish or listening to your first singing Northern Cardinal of the year are all things that can make us just happy to be alive. Simply just watching, observing, and enjoying birds is really all we need, but lucky for us, there is even more to it.

For many of us, the most exciting moment in birding is finding a rare bird. While there are various weather conditions that can increase our chances of predicting where and when to potentially find a rare bird, it is still a long shot. Birding local patches routinely and putting the time in is a great strategy. This may be cliche, but nature is always full of surprises and the more time spent outdoors, the more surprises one will experience.

Our process geared towards taking the risk out early really set us up well heading into spring migration. We always knew which expected species we needed to target and when to target them. We were relentless in the "first winter" of the year to make sure we hit our targets so that we were in good shape for spring. Not only did we hit our targets, but we exceeded them. We even had many of our birds pegged for October and November already behind us. The goal was to be able to spend as much time as possible in the field birding during peak migrations without having to worry about "birds of need" piling up on our to-do list. If we had to play catch up in the heart of spring migration, we would have been minimizing our likelihood of finding our own goodies. We could not afford sacrificing opportunity. Even if we only turned up a couple of rare birds of our own, that could have a significant impact in a Big Year.

On April 25, we were out birding by a small lake and were enjoying a nice influx of Swamp Sparrows, Ruby-crowned Kinglets, Yellow-rumped and Palm Warblers. Slowly working the edge of the lake, we suddenly had a large rail flush from less than ten feet away and it flew into some dense vegetation maybe fifty feet further out into the lake. We clearly saw a dark rail with a mostly red bill and white flank stripe. This was a Common Gallinule! This species is a rare breeder in Maine and most years would involve driving two hours, then taking a canoe or kayak out and hoping that you hear one with no guarantee. We knew this was a big-time find for our Big Year and that more time would now be opened up for our future birding.

One week later on May 2nd, we were birding a local marsh promptly after sunrise. As we walked towards the end of the forest trail that leads to the marshy edge, a very small wading bird flushed from a juniper patch. The bird flew away from us, quickly banked right, and disappeared. While our view of the bird was mainly looking down at its back, the combination of navy blue and buffy tan to buffy orange could only be one thing. It was a Least Bittern! This is another tough-to-find bird in Maine and typically requires a lot of effort with no guarantees. While we did just happen upon the bittern, we happened upon it due to our effort and time spent in the field. This time was opened up thanks to our Integrated Birding Process.

We already shared the story of the Tufted Puffin that we spotted cruising by Dyer Point in Cape Elizabeth on May 22. This bird warrants another quick mention here as it was part of an important chain of events, kind of like our own Big Year version of the Patagonia Picnic Table Effect. If we didn't find our own Common Gallinule, maybe we would have been chasing one on the day we found the Least Bittern, and therefore, not seen the bittern. If we didn't see the Least Bittern, maybe we would have been chasing one on the day we saw the Tufted Puffin instead of seeing the puffin. If we didn't see the Tufted Puffin, there would have been no garlic green beans. And so on and so on. All of these sightings and the green beans were the result of The Experiment working its magic.

The Tufted Puffin, without a doubt, was our craziest self-found vagrant. Next on this list, happened in the fall. It was November. It was a Sunday. And it came true.

November means one thing to most birdwatchers. Rarity season! Early November is prime time for vagrancy and notoriously some big-time rarities show up in this timeframe. The reasons for this are extremely varied, but things such as reverse migration (birds that fly north instead of south) and birds of western North America riding the prevailing westerly winds to the east are a couple of examples. Many of the migrants in the fall are young birds that were just born in the same summer and are making their first big trip. Add in that much of the continent is undergoing seasonal landscape changes impacting food sources and you have birds on the move. The possibilities are endless.

On November 1st, an annual vagrant on our original target list of 302 species finally showed up. Two Eurasian Wigeons were reported in Cumberland county in the early afternoon. Noah was busy working on a time sensitive outdoor home project that needed to get done, so he could not go. Stacey decided to go ahead, alone, to see the wigeons. Now remember, this Big Year was a true team effort and we agreed that both of us had to see or hear each bird for us to be able to count it. For that reason, Stacey did not submit an eBird list for her Eurasian

Wigeon sighting right away. We had to cross our fingers wicked haahd in hopes that the wigeons would stay and that Noah could see them on the following morning.

Noah went the next morning (Sunday, November 2) to where the wigeons were reported and unexpectedly found a maze of ponds. There were a couple of different trails through forest that could access different areas. It was not possible to view all of the ponds from a single vantage point. After an hour and a half of searching, Noah finally located the wigeons in the last possible location. It was a very small and sheltered pond, requiring the full hike to view. This was bird #320 for the year.

Stacey was waiting for Noah at her "secret" birding spot in her hometown. This location is small, quiet, and located right next to a river. In the fall, the habitat is open and mainly consists of patches of thickets. This was a location that Noah was never excited to bird during peak migration because it is not super diverse typically, but it is a lovely place. At about 10:00am, Noah arrived and met Stacey at the bench by the river. This was our opportunity to fill in our eBird checklists with the Eurasian Wigeons and submit them. As we filled out our checklists, we started discussing where we were going to bird next. Then Noah started hearing a chip note. He first brushed it off as a distant Yellow-rumped Warbler. Then heard it again and thought, Common Yellowthroat? It was too sharp for a Yellowthroat and too sharp for a Yellow-rumped. It chipped again and we were confused by the call. Noah walked over towards the brushy island in the middle of the park about 100 feet from our bench. Hearing the chip some more was even more confusing. To Noah, the chip was somewhere in between a Yellow-rumped Warbler and a Northern Cardinal. Closer to the cardinal call, but not a cardinal.

Stacey heard Noah say "Ohhhh" and quickly caught up with him. At first, a brief view of the bird indicated a sparrow-sized warbler with a grey hood and lots of bright yellow underneath from the chest to the undertail. There was an uncertain amount of white around the eye.

Three warblers fit this general look; Mourning Warbler, Connecticut Warbler, and MacGillivray's Warbler. Mourning Warblers breed in Maine, but November is very late for them. Connecticut Warblers breed in the northern regions of the Great Lakes, as well as Canada. In Maine, they are a very tough-to-find fall migrant. MacGillivray's Warblers are a western bird that breed in extreme western Canada and the western quarter or so of the United States. Up to this point, there had only been 6 accepted records of MacGillivray's in Maine.

The bird was still chipping constantly and we knew this chip was different from the more familiar Mourning and Connecticut. Neither of us had any experience with a MacGillivray's, so doubt naturally crept in. This bird piqued our curiosity!

We continued stalking the bird and recorded plenty of audio recordings, but we were still trying to get a clear view for photos. We knew we needed photos of this bird not only for evidence, but for identification as well. Capturing a photo was challenging because the bird was only intermittently visible and moving quickly through dense brush. After what seemed like an eternity, the warbler chipped its way up a short tree and came almost into full view, but still obscured. We both got some photos at that point that looked promising. We quickly eliminated Connecticut Warbler as this bird did not have the bold full eyering that a Connecticut would show. This warbler had a broken eyering that was not connected in front of or behind the eye. Young Mourning Warblers have a broken eye ring, but it is very narrow. Also the throat and the area above the lores (feathers between the eye and bill) on Mourning should be yellowish. "Our bird" had bold eye arcs that appeared broader and shorter than is typical of a young Mourning Warbler. It also showed a pale whitish throat and pale whitish supraloral area (above the lores). Did we really just find Maine's 7th MacGillivray's Warbler?

After the bird stopped chipping and moved deeper into the thicket, we sat back down on the bench to gather ourselves. The adrenaline was pumping and we knew that we probably had a MacGillivray's Warbler, but couldn't really believe it. It's times like these where it is better to let cooler heads be the judge and what better people than experts like Derek, Alex, and Louis. Noah sent a back-of-camera photo to them and they all came back with "MacGillivray's!!!" Big Year bird #321 and a lifer for both. Wow!

We quickly sent the word out to the Maine rare bird group chat. Within 30 minutes of posting, birders started funneling in to see this bird. It was great to see so many people excited to see this super rare bird for our state. "Mac" stuck around for the rest of November and well over one hundred birders got to see it, much to the dismay of Stacey having to advertise her secret birding spot.

This bird will always be a special memory for us. As much as the process of The Experiment created our opportunity to find Mac, other variables were at play. If we both saw the Eurasian Wigeons on the previous day, we likely never would have ended up at the secret spot. Much like the Spruce Grouse and the Tufted Puffin, there was certainly an element of divine intervention, but hard work, planning, and passing the berry led us down that path. Another Sunday, another come true.

Top: Common Gallinule; Bottom: MacGillivray's Warbler

Top and Bottom: Cave Swallow

323

After tying the previous Maine Big Year record on November 3rd, we began to set our sights on the next target, the record setter. But which bird would be the record setter? It seemed to be a common topic amongst ourselves and other birders. It was fun to contemplate. Since November is known as rarity season, pretty much anything can show up. So how could we possibly know what bird the record setter would be? The answer, we couldn't, at least not without listening to the wind first.

Late October to mid November is prime time for Cave Swallow vagrancy in the northeast. There is a Caribbean population of Cave Swallow, but the majority of this species and the few that make it to the northeast, are presumably the birds from Mexico. The Mexican breeding population has expanded north into the southern U.S. and are now breeding in Texas and New Mexico. Every fall, strong winds from low pressure weather systems push some of these birds north, often as far as the Great Lakes of the United States. Then strong westerly winds sweep them eastward to the northeast coast. Weather forecasts were showing some very strong NW winds for November 5th-7th here in Maine. We knew what this meant. The wind was speaking to us.

When prime wind conditions and the right time of year collide, does it mean you are guaranteed to see Cave Swallows? Absolutely not, but it is probably close to a guarantee that someone will see one, somewhere. To give some perspective, Noah had been scouring coastlines for about 20 years under the proper conditions and had never hit the jackpot.

We checked some great coastal areas of southern Maine such as Fort Foster on November 5th, but no Cave Swallows. We went back out on November 6th and did it again in some different coastal hot spots and also came up empty. In this time period, a few birders had seen Cave Swallows, but we simply were not in the right place at the right time. With more strong NW winds predicted on November 7th, coupled with a reported sighting from late afternoon on the 6th, we decided to get back to Fort Foster first thing in the morning.

Fort Foster is located in Kittery at the southern tip of Maine and is a south pointing peninsula. This geography is perfect for concentrating migrants in the fall. Migrant birds are hesitant to cross the Piscataqua River to continue on to New Hampshire after a long night or day of migration. Swallows are strong flyers, however, and don't really have an issue crossing water in most cases. We still felt like this location would give us the best chance of stumbling into a Cave Swallow. One reason is that any swallows pushed to the coast should eventually head south and what better place is there to be but at the southernmost point of our state. Another theory we tossed around was that if the swallows were hungry and arrived at Fort Foster, they likely wouldn't continue to cross the expanse of water south to New Hampshire without hunting "the fort" first. This could lead to a potential "concentration" of Cave Swallows, even if it was just one. Now the wind had told us where to go.

It was a warm day and quite enjoyable if one was protected from the wind. We had stationed ourselves in the southeast corner of the park but of course, had seen zero Cave Swallows in the first hour. We ran into a local birding friend, Magill, who mentioned that someone had seen a dozen swallows there the afternoon prior. There had to be at least one still here, right? Then a photographer walked up to us and said, "Did you see the swallow?" What? Where? The photographer pointed and we did not hesitate.

We rapidly moved to the most northeastern stretch of coastline on the property as this was where the dozen birds were the night before. There was a nice warm microclimate happening due to this area being sheltered from wind. We scanned the rocks and looked for flying birds but no sign of any swallows. We felt dejected. Magill headed back south and said she would call if she saw one.

Only a couple of minutes later, as we had turned around to walk back, Magill phoned Stacey. "Magill has the bird!" Stacey said to Noah. We both ran as fast as we could. Mind you, the two of us running fast uphill and 11 months into a Big Year was not fast at all, and was quite painful.

It felt like an eternity running the 200 feet or so up the hill, but alas, we saw Magill taking photos pointing towards the rocks in between her and the ocean. Then we saw the Cave Swallow perched on a rock. It was beautiful! And we did it! We set a new state record! And with a lifer! This was Big Year bird number 323. It was an emotionally charged moment, one that is hard to describe with words. We spent some quality time photographing the vagrant swallow. The sunlight was perfect and the bird was more than cooperative, allowing us super close views on the rocks as well as low and slow passes in flight as it foraged for insects. Certainly one of the cutest birds of the year! We will let the photos tell the rest of the story.

A BIRD IN THE HAND

In early May, we were sitting in the car watching the birdfeeders in the side yard at Brendan's house. He had reported a visiting Summer Tanager. With his permission, we enjoyed the gorgeous tanager. While sipping our coffee, our calm and relaxed morning soon turned to high energy. A rare bird alert was just posted in the chat group. As luck would have it, the tanager and the now new rare bird were in the same town - we were minutes away from a rarity!

The rare bird alert indicated a Worm-eating Warbler had just been banded at the local bird banding facility. We went right over. We were there to watch as the bird was being measured and delicately examined. We were able to take photos of the warbler while it was held by one of the researchers. Then, the researcher let it fly free. It flew deep into the brush without stopping. We never saw it again, despite a second visit to the site later that day.

This was a tough one. An opportunity, but a netted, banded, then released bird. Worm-eating Warbler was not one of our 302 annual Maine birds, but a vagrant. It would have been a lifer for Stacey and a Maine state bird for Noah. The bird banding facility does important research and in an ethical manner. As birders in the midst of a Big

Year, we were faced with a dilemma. Here was a bird that never showed us itself in its natural, unrestrained state. Like many other birding topics, "natural" can be interpreted differently by different birders. That is fine. Scenarios are variable and we each need to make decisions based on what we know to be true. Additionally, there are some written rules by birding organizations that lay out guidelines for when to count birds.[3,4] After much back and forth, we decided that since we did not see the bird in its natural state *after* it was released, we would not count it toward our Big Year. At the onset of our Big Year, we both agreed that we wanted an indisputable final species list with no question marks hovering over any reports. Fact is, if the bird was not netted, it would have been highly unlikely that we would have seen it. The banded bird was the only Worm-eating warbler we saw in 2025.

Worm-eating Warbler; photo credit S.P.Huth

THE PHOTOS TELL THE STORY

We hope you enjoyed the stories from this section of the book.

Our Big Year was filled with so many more stories and thousands of photographs. On many occasions, the photos alone tell the story. With that, rather than carry on with words, please enjoy some of our Big Year moments with these favorite images.

- A magical day with a vagrant Black-necked Stilt in Belfast;
- A sunny afternoon at Timber Point with a Buff-breasted Sandpiper;
- A day with Purple Sandpipers at the Rockland Jetty;
- Eagle watching in Knox;
- A morning at Capisic Park with many Warblers: Northern Parula, Chestnut-sided, Black-throated Blue, Northern Yellow, Bay-breasted, and Yellow-rumped;
- A drive north to Mount Desert Island to see a Red-headed Woodpecker;
- A Snow Bunting on the rocks in Kittery;
- Low tide at Biddeford Pool with an American Oystercatcher;
- Evening Grosbeak at a residence in York;
- White-winged Dove in a Portland neighborhood;
- An active Hooded Warbler in Biddeford;

* All photos taken by Noah Gibb, except where indicated otherwise.

Top: Black-necked Stilt; Bottom: Buff-breasted Sandpiper

Top: Purple Sandpiper; Bottom: Bald Eagle

Top: Northern Parula; Bottom: Chestnut-sided Warbler

Top: Black-throated Blue Warbler; Bottom: Northern Yellow Warbler

Top: Bay-breasted Warbler; Bottom: Yellow-rumped Warbler

Top: Red-headed Woodpecker, photo credit S.P.Huth; Bottom: Snow Bunting

Top: American Oystercatcher, photo credit S.P.Huth; Bottom: Evening Grosbeak

Top: White-winged Dove, photo credit S.P.Huth; Bottom: Hooded Warbler;

Vesper Sparrow

3

THE OUTCOME

You guessed it! By the end of our Maine Big Year, we recorded 332 species and surpassed the prior state record of 322. While we did anticipate that The Experiment would require commitment, we truly did not understand the magnitude of the commitment. Frankly, by the time May rolled around, we had so much time and energy invested, there was no way we would give in nor give up to the fatigue, occasional disappointments or life pressures. Noah was balancing family needs, a full time job, and Noah's Birding Tours. From June through August, Stacey was battling sciatica and at times struggled with sitting, standing and walking. Despite the challenges, we focused on the goal. Remember, too, that we had no overnight birding excursions. We traveled to our destinations, and then back to our respective homes, all within the day. Our longest "day" was 20 hours.

Maine is a big state to cover with day trips. We both live in the southern part of the state. Starting from our meeting place at the Yarmouth park-n-ride, it is possible to drive 7 hours to the far reaches of Maine. There are 16 counties, with some rural areas that have precarious logging roads and few human inhabitants. We covered all 16 counties, with eBird checklists for each. For some regions, we relied on intel from fellow birders in order to streamline the driving events. That said, there were many long trips. Some trips were well worth the effort, others not so much.

Regardless of the drive time, the challenges for each bird varied. We already discussed the effort required for Spruce Grouse and Glaucous Gull. There are multiple other examples of some high effort and challenging birds. Bicknell's Thrush is known to nest in the timberline of the Krummholz zone. In Maine, this zone is located at elevations of about 3500 - 4000 ft. At the end of May, the air temperature is heating up and the black flies are swarming and vicious. Our trip up to the Krummholz zone on May 28 was brutal. All for a bird. We climbed up the 4000 ft mountain, saw and photographed the bird, and then proceeded to hobble back down a steep descent. The ordeal was nearly crippling and marked the onset of Stacey's sciatica. Was all of this worth it for one bird? Not exactly. Fortunately, in addition to Bicknell's, we also had good looks at a Boreal Chickadee. So, yeah, it was worth the effort.

In mid-July,` we also had an interesting chase requiring substantial endurance. We set off on the Dunstan River in a canoe to find a reported Seaside Sparrow. Typically, this would not have been a big deal. However, this was during the sciatica peak. Sitting on a hard canoe bench and hunched over while paddling and juggling a camera added additional challenges to the already physically painful expedition. Was all of this pain worth seeing an obscured glimpse of a stealthy Seaside Sparrow as it peeked out amongst the marsh grass? We endured the greenhead fly bites, snapped the photo and paddled away.

Another example of serious effort was not as fruitful as Bicknell's and Seaside. We had been searching potential roosting areas, unsuccessfully, for Long-eared Owl. By the end of December, we had little time left to find this elusive species of owl and decided to pull out all the stops. Parts of Maine succumbed to heavy snowfall over the holidays which hampered accessibility to promising areas where owls may hunt at dark. We set off for one last try by bundling up in our warmest gear while donning snowshoes and headlamps for a night expedition. Unfortunately, 2025 would come to a close with Stacey still not having seen a Long-eared Owl, and with Noah still missing this bird on his Maine state list. Regardless, the effort was worth the memory of a pristine habitat in the Maine winter.

Our Integrated Birding Process and our philosophy of taking the risk out early amounted to 100 species by the end of January. By the end of May we had 259 species. The remaining 73 species were spread through the last seven months. Refer to Figure 1.

Figure 1. Cumulative Bird Species by Month

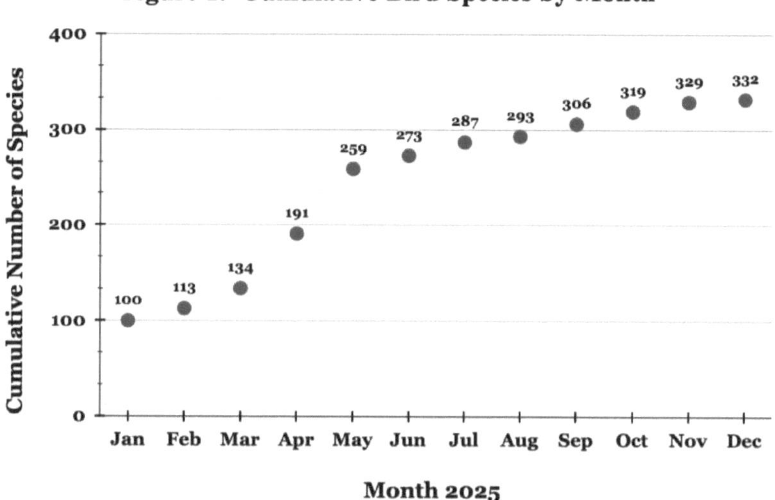

What was the make-up of the 332 species we observed in the Big Year? Figure 2 shows the three categories of birds we outlined in The Experiment chapter. Depending on the source used, the number of species making a regular appearance in Maine varies. Based on our birding experience, we settled on 302 expected species. We considered these 302 species annual migrants passing through Maine, or breeding species that nest in Maine. In the end, we reported 292 of the 302 expected annual migrants or breeding birds. We missed only 10 species from our targeted 302. The remaining 40 species from our overall total of 332 were vagrants. Vagrants were any species that were reported in Maine in 2025 that were not typically annual migrants or breeders in the state.

Figure 2. 332 Species for Our Maine Big Year 2025

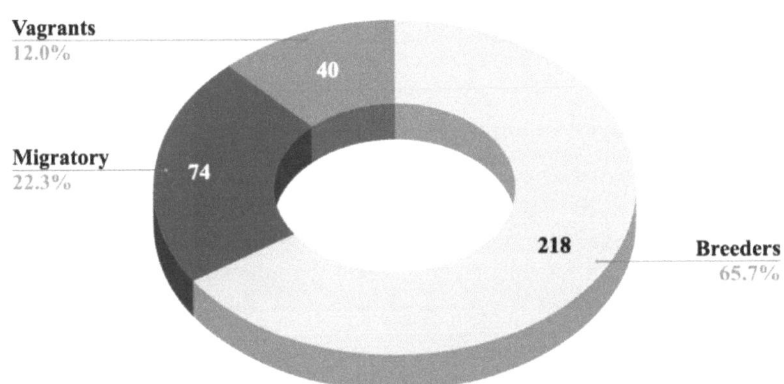

The next graph, in Figure 3, illustrates the power of our Integrated Birding Process. Recall the twelve-tab spreadsheet in The Experiment chapter. For each month of the year, we identified and listed the 302 birds we would target during their earliest anticipated month. The dotted line in the graph depicts the plan. The 302 annual species expected over the course of the year are shown cumulatively. Superimposed, are the actual data depicted by the solid line. The actual data, or the 292 annual species observed, are also represented cumulatively over the twelve months.

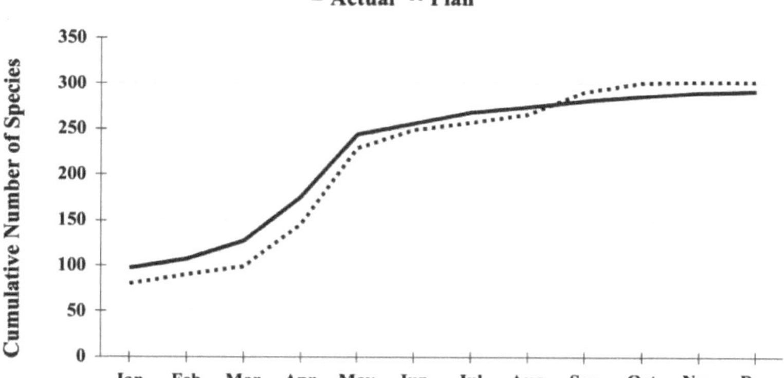

The outcome of the data in Figure 3 is an interesting area for discussion. For the first three quarters of the year, the actual data exceeded the plan. We intentionally designed our process to accelerate sightings earlier in the year by targeting birds that required effort in the earliest months possible. This approach kept us focused, and turned out to be a smart decision. The graph illustrates the magnitude of our focus by showing that the *actual* data trendline was consistently at a higher cumulative species count than the *plan* through August. At that point, the trendlines crossover. It was the accelerated pace of the annual bird findings prior to the crossover point that allowed for time to observe vagrants in the last quarter of the year. The strategy worked. Our plan was validated. The accelerated delivery of species by our plan was evidenced by the "actual" data. Further validation was proven by The Experiment outcome, a new state record was set. Now, look at the vagrant chart in Figure 4.

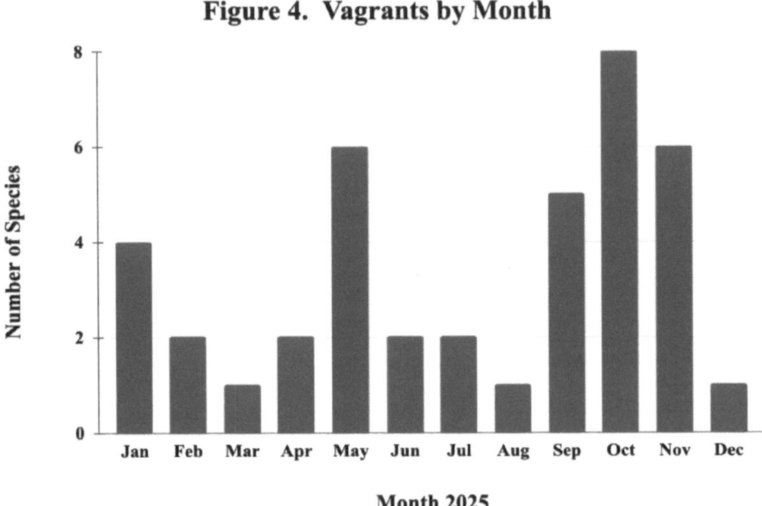

Yes, we had vagrants all months of the year. However, 50% of the vagrants we observed were in the last four months of the year. If we had to drive, locate, and identify a larger portion of the annual 302 species toward the end of the year, well who knows how many vagrants we may have missed? We designed, developed and executed The Experiment to plan, as intended, and ended the Big Year with a whopping 332 species.

We logged 35,000 miles of driving. Noah did at least 95% of the driving. Wait. While Noah was driving, Stacey did the research, documentation, navigation and provided the unstoppable banter. As a team, we recognized early on that our roles, in parallel, were essential to our ability to deliver 332 species in day trips and with limitations to our schedules. Teamwork turned out to be key to the successful Experiment, just as we predicted.

Our car time was important for planning, and that allowed for productive birding once we were at our destination. By the time we arrived in Aroostook County, for example, we knew what specific locations we needed to go to, what targets we needed to see, and how long it would take to get from site to site. We knew when to lug our scopes, when there was time to grab a bite to eat versus only time for an apple, or when we could make it back to the Brunswick airport in time to look for Short-eared Owls at dusk. Our planning, strategy, and individual roles became second nature, and it worked.

We birded approximately 300 days in the year, with an average birding day equivalent to 5 hours. We logged about 1500 hours, including driving time. Given the 332 species we reported, the math calculates to about 100 miles and 4.5 hours per bird. The habitats we enjoyed along the way were as diverse as the bird species themselves. By far, one of the most remarkable habitat experiences occurred in the North Maine Woods. We appreciated relief from artificial sounds. There was no noise from lawnmowers, leaf blowers or traffic jams. There was no rumbling noise from airplanes or passing cars. There was no cell signal which meant our phones were quiet. This left us with only the sounds of nature. We arrived in the North Woods feeling frazzled from The Experiment, but we left this habitat of solitude feeling refreshed.

The first priority in our list of must-haves was to enjoy the experience. For us, the critical piece here was finding birds rather than chasing. Finding birds meant that we found target species, but also found species that were unexpected. For example, a trip to a location just a couple of miles from our houses resulted in the expected shorebirds, but we also unexpectedly flushed a Least Bittern. There had been no prior reports of the bittern. We did not target the bittern, but there it was. This also happens to be one of the 14 birds for which we were unable to capture photo or audio evidence. We simply could not reflex in enough time to grab a photo. The sighting, though, was pure enjoyment at that moment, and we talked about the event for days after.

The flip-side was chasing. Rare birds that are found and reported by other birders are most certainly desired when the goal is to rack up as many species as possible. We were up in Washington county when the report came in that an American Avocet was foraging in a marsh in the southernmost county, York. We were actually finishing up one of our many Spruce Grouse expeditions when the Avocet eBird rare bird alert came through. There was almost no discussion needed. We immediately started the five hour drive back south. We arrived at the specified location with enough daylight to walk the path to the marsh. Just as the weather shifted to drizzling rain, there it was. We did it. We saw the Avocet. Took the photos, blurry from the rain. Then, we dragged ourselves back to the car. Well, that was great to see an Avocet, a vagrant in Maine. Not so sure we would define it as fun. Traveling to see birds identified by other birders, especially when the drive is significant, is a must when participating in a Big Year. Some birders love the chase. For us, it became more of a necessary chore. That said, we were fortunate and grateful to have other birders taking photos and expeditiously reporting their finds. We recognize this as a critical ingredient to a successful Big Year. After all was said and done, our travel log indicates we spent approximately 15% of our total time (including driving) dedicated to *chasing* birds. In advance of the Big Year, we had no way to estimate how the unpredictable chase-time would add up. The 15% of time invested in chasing seemed like a worthy and reasonable trade off, leaving 85% of our time focused on *finding* birds.

Continuing with the "finding joy" theme, our strategy outlined typical habitats for each species, alongside the earliest time of year we could expect to find the species. The purpose of that methodology was twofold. First, we wanted to gain efficiency. With limited time, it was important to "batch" as many targets as possible for every birding event. We did gain efficiency, as evidenced by the species per month graph, shown in Figure 1. With early momentum in the first part of the year, we were able to accomplish the second purpose, which was joy. The last three or four months of the year became as much about where we *wanted* to go versus where we *had* to go to find targets. By default, our days became less complicated and more closely resembling a non-Big Year extravaganza. We were less pressured to find target birds, and instead had the mindset to notice the beauty of Washington County or the intense eyes of a Northern Mockingbird. We stopped and watched the deer herds in Hancock County and took in the sights and sounds along the rocky coast and the boreal forest. The Big Year transitioned to being pleasurable rather than an intense yearning for a new bird, as long as Noah was back in time to grab pizza from his favorite shop on Saturday. All bets were off if he couldn't make it in time.

Our self-imposed expectation to accompany our eBird checklists with diagnostic evidence for each new species was pretty high. We included either photos, audios, or both for more than 96% of our birds. As described earlier, good documentation gives credibility to the sighting and to the birder, which also provides the eBird reviewers adequate justification to confirm. We also recognize there are times when a photo or audio is not possible. Some birds or situations simply do not present themselves in a way that allows for best-practice documentation.

Additionally, we were 100% determined to ensure we *both* saw or heard every species. We did. For the large majority, we were together at the same time, as our eBird checklists indicate. However, on a few occasions, we documented species separately. In advance of The Experiment, we agreed no checklists would be submitted for new species until (or unless) we both experienced the bird. For example, Stacey had an Orange-crowned Warbler in her backyard. She did not submit that eBird checklist until Noah saw the warbler a few weeks later. Occasionally, we discussed the what-if scenario of a rare bird flyover when only one of us was present. This was a point of contention, but fortunately that scenario did not play out for us in 2025. We ended the Big Year each with the same number of species.

Of the 302 annual species we targeted for our Maine Big Year, we missed 10. These species were either a) not reported (and perhaps not seen); b) seen but not reported in a timely manner; c) reported but we were unsuccessful in the chase; or d) reported flyovers and not chaseable. Figure 5 shows the 10 missed annual species:

Figure 5. Our Big Year 2025 "Misses"

		Not Reported	Seen, Not Reported in a timely manner	Reported, unsuccessfully chased by us	Reported Flyovers
1	Mute Swan	X			
2	Chuck-will's-widow	X			
3	Marbled Godwit	X			
4	Sabine's Gull		X		
5	Long-eared Owl		X		
6	American Three-toed Woodpecker			X	
7	Long-tailed Jaeger			X	
8	South Polar Skua			X	
9	Royal Tern				X
10	White-winged Crossbill				X

Finally, recall that vagrant species made up the balance of our total species count of 332. Our hard work, planning and team collaboration paid off as we observed and documented 75% of the vagrants that were reported in Maine in 2025.

Demonstrating good leadership behavior in our birding community was another goal. We were committed to being good stewards. At times, it can be hard to do what is best for the broader team versus oneself. We do not claim to have accomplished our leadership goal all of the time, but we sure did try. We routinely submitted our eBird checklists right away, typically as soon as we returned to the car and before arriving at the next birding spot. We also reported interesting and/or rare finds on the state and local chat groups. Initially, we reported in a timely fashion in order to assist our fellow birders and friends see more birds. While that was a likely outcome, what became more evident was how our rapid reporting was met with rapid reporting directly back to us from others. We started to receive more texts and emails from folks trying to assist us in finding targets. They had no idea if we had already seen the species, but no matter, the fact that others were selflessly giving back to us was refreshing and valued tremendously. We came to refer to this reciprocation phenomenon as "passing the berry." Frugivore species, such as Cedar Waxwings, are known for mating rituals that include one of the pair picking a berry. The berry-picker will court its potential mate by passing the berry. Together, they pass the berry back and forth, as though they are gifting each other. When we reported a bird, and others then reciprocated with their intel, we experienced joy from the practice of passing the berry! This was a humbling reminder of what matters. It's not always just about the birds.

The integrated process of creating the plan using spreadsheets of targets, timing and locations was as important as working as a team. At any given time, we had real-time knowledge of what we reported, what remained to be seen and when, and every gap that we had to fill. Out in the field, we were routinely asked "What do you still need?" We were able to rattle off the list instantly. Why? Because while one of us was contemplating pizza, the other had the real-time Google Drive spreadsheet application open on their phone.

Along with the integrated process of The Experiment, some other routines became apparent as we delivered our Big Year. Here are a few:

1. Morning coffee from the drive through. Aside from fuel for the car, this was our biggest expense. The greeting from the drive through attendant became a must-have to start the day.
2. After every new "year bird" we gave each other a high five. Sometimes we gave high fives twice because we could not remember if we already did.
3. The snack bag. We had peanut butter crackers, trail mix, dried fruit and fresh fruit stashed in the back seat. It was imperative to keep the snack bag stocked, and also transferred to whatever car we used that day.
4. The clipboard. It was in the car and held all the integrated process spreadsheets developed for The Experiment. While

traveling to our next birding spot, Stacey updated the spreadsheets about every other day and read the gaps out loud for team review. This was a key element to help keep us on track and focused.

5. During return car rides, we frequently called Stacey's brother on speaker phone. Steve is a non-birder, and was supportive and genuinely excited every time we raised the bar and/or had new birds. He readily absorbed and contributed thoughts to the strategy and regularly said "I think The Experiment is workiiing!"

Collectively, these small but important habits became essential for success.

By the end of 2025, we were co-leaders in creating a new high record for the number of species seen in the state of Maine, 332. We also set a new annual record for the number of species seen in Cumberland County, in Southern Maine, 265. This is the county in which we both live. The county record was not accomplished by design, but was a nice unintended consequence of our hard work and planning, and a wonderful bonus. It is important to mention that the state and county annual record-holders that came before us did the hard work, too. They likely experienced the fatigue and stress that accompanies lofty missions. Their contributions and accomplishments are not minimized by new records being set. We stood on their shoulders. Someday, when our records are broken, we can only hope that our efforts will be appreciated and that their good leadership will set an example for how extreme birding can be both successful and enjoyable.

*Facing Page: Northern Parula; Next Page: Black-necked Stilt, photo credit S.P.Huth

4

THE TAKEAWAYS

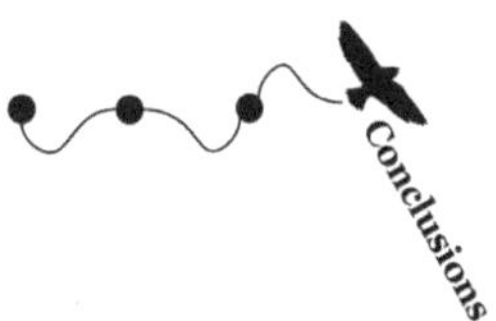

At the end of a long but short birding year, we paused and celebrated our accomplishment. Pizza may have been involved. Next, we reflected. What did we learn? What were our takeaways? This chapter serves to share some of the lessons we learned, and with the hope that the messages put forth are interpreted with the spirit of continuous improvement in mind.

We pulled our learnings together and built a formula that we believe conveys how we maximized our species count. Refer to Figure 6.

Figure 6. Our Formula

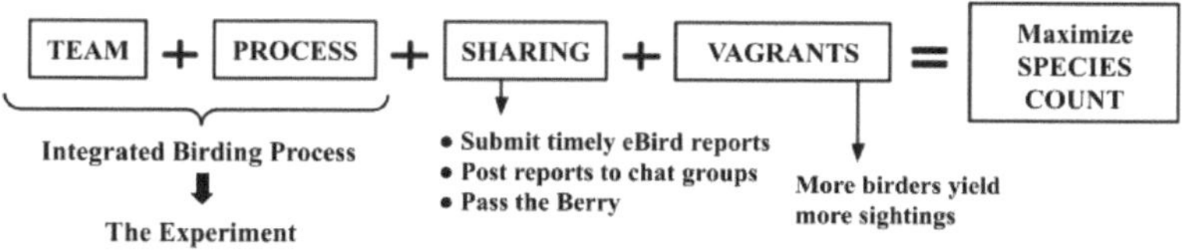

We've already covered the benefits of both team collaboration and practicing the Integrated Birding Process as defined by The Experiment. The Process must be well executed. Our real-time approach carefully incorporated taking the risk out early so that we could minimize missed opportunities later. In particular, we frequently balanced the time required for chasing versus finding. If not, one risk becomes missing vagrants in order to fill gaps left by delayed sightings of annual birds.

In addition to Team and Process components, Sharing and Vagrants are the other variables included in the formula. We knew we would routinely share our bird findings with the birding community in as close to real-time as possible. However, what we did not anticipate was the boost in *our* species count as a result of our sharing (leadership). Passing the Berry was one form of sharing and was not only a contributor to our success, but it showed the goodness of how the birding community became our supporters and how birders supported each other. Finally, vagrants comprised just under 12% of our annual species count. Which vagrants and where they land and when they may arrive are not predictable. This is where more people birding can be most helpful for maximizing a Big Year. First, the vagrants must be sighted. More people birding can help boost the likelihood vagrants will be found. Then, more sightings can lead to more reports. More reports that contain photo or audio evidence can be confirmed. The outcome may be a higher annual species count.

In addition to the formula, there are a couple of other topics to discuss. On multiple occasions over the course of the year, some birders would suggest to us that there are more species of birds in Maine now versus the last 15 years. The implication may have been that we were racking up species, in part, because it was now easier. It is true that more people are seeing more birds in Maine.[5] The number of people participating in birding, especially since the COVID pandemic era, has increased. Tools like eBird, Merlin, and chat groups have likely facilitated the ease with which sightings are communicated, enabling more people to see more birds.

Further, social media is another outlet that has ramped up communication relative to 15 years ago. Often, a homeowner with a smart bird feeder does not know what species they had at their feeder. They do know it was different from what they typically see. They post the images and almost instantly they learn it is a rare bird for their region. Within an hour they have birders reaching out requesting if they can hang out to watch their feeder. When all is said and done, and even with advancements in communication and identification tools, we do not believe there are statistically more *species* in Maine now versus 15 years ago. That is not to say more species may not someday expand into Maine, similar to the Red-bellied Woodpecker.[6] However, both the increasing and decreasing of species is confounded by multiple variables. Simple statements such as "there are more species now in Maine" minimize a complex dynamic.

For example, 30 years ago, only about a dozen Eastern Bluebirds were spotted during the annual Maine Audubon Christmas Bird Count.[7] Today, the bluebird population has greatly increased. They are numerous and can be observed all year in regions of Maine. Conservation efforts and bluebird nest boxes are two factors that contributed to their recovery. This example illustrates that at times a species may have low prevalence in a region, however the trend can shift, and for any number of reasons. Conversely, a bird species may shift from a higher prevalence to a lower prevalence in a region. An example of a declining species in Maine can be cited by reviewing the Audubon Christmas Bird Count data for Glaucous Gull.[7] Over the past 20+ years Glaucous Gulls have become more challenging to find, likely due to multiple factors including climate change. Another example is Pine Grosbeak. These frugivores are rarely reported in Maine during winters when there are limited crab apples and Mountain Ash berries available in the state. When fruit supply is plentiful north of Maine, the frugivores generally remain in the north. However, when fruit supplies are inadequate north of Maine AND in good supply in Maine, the frugivores spread south to Maine. In fact, we targeted Pine Grosbeak as a February bird in our Big Year. The fruity food supply in

Maine was low in winter '24/'25. However, in November, we recorded a Pine Grosbeak in the southernmost county of Maine. Why? This is because in the winter of '25/'26 the fruit supply was very good in Maine, and low in regions north of Maine. The takeaway with these examples is that many factors that enable or inhibit movement of birds are in fact variable. The birds will come to Maine when the conditions are right and not necessarily because there is a shift in number of species.

To drive this point home, Figure 7 shows eBird data from years dating back to 2010. We used eBird data because it is public information and easily accessible. A reminder, the extracted eBird data included here was from 12.31.25. In the graph, the total number of species confirmed each year (denoted by •) is plotted alongside the number of species reported by the top ranked eBirder for that year (denoted by ■). The data shows that in order for new records to be set, a birder must report a large percentage of the confirmed species for that year. Look at 2011, for example. There were 332 species confirmed, with the top eBirder reporting 314 species (or 94.6%). Compare that with just a year earlier, 2010. There were 333 species confirmed, with 282 reported by the top eBirder, for 84.7%. The difference between 2010 and 2011 is not because the number of species in Maine were different. In fact, they were statistically identical. Of further interest, the same birder was ranked at the top in both 2010 and 2011. We do not claim to know or understand the complex variables between the two years. However, we do know the number of species and the birder were the same (yes, the birder gained a year of experience from 2010 to 2011, which is not to be minimized). We would surmise that the birder exerted significantly more effort in 2011 versus 2010. What an impressive accomplishment and kudos to doing what it takes to raise the bar. It is hard work. As evidenced by the year over year comparison date, the record was not broken in 2011 because there were more species of birds in Maine.

Figure 7. Confirmed Species and Species for Top eBirder

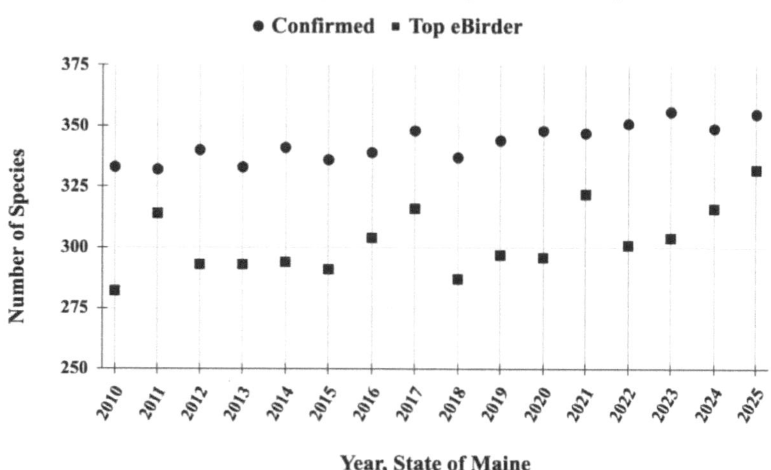

Look at another example shown in Figure 7. Compare 2021 and 2022. In 2021, the prior state record of 316 was broken with an impressive total of 322 species reported. That year, 347 species of birds were confirmed. Therefore, the top eBirder reported 92.8% of the confirmed species. The next year of 2022, and the same top eBirder, reported 85.8% (or 301 species of 351 confirmed). Yes, some years are better than others due to weather, personal circumstances, variable number of species on pelagics, variation of food sources, vagrant findings and so on. That said, the number of bird species in Maine has not been a barrier to breaking records, to date. We produced 332 species in our Maine Big Year in 2025, in a year that had 355 confirmed species as of 12.31.25. That translates to reporting 93.5% of the confirmed species! Hard. Work.

Speaking of some years being better than others, let's discuss vagrants. Refer again to Figure 7. It is obvious that had Noah and Stacey done their Big Year in 2015, the outcome may have been different. Wait! Noah was the top eBirder in 2015. That year, 336 species were reported and confirmed in Maine. In fact, he reported 274 annual birds and 17 vagrants, for a total of 291 species. In 2015, in order to report 332 species like we did in 2025, he would have needed to spot >98% of the 336 species. That scenario seems improbable just by looking at the face value of needing to sight almost every bird that year. Therefore, having a year with enough reported and confirmed species is imperative if the desire is to set new records. Unfortunately, we cannot know what the total number of species will be until the end of the year. If we assume the expected annual species were equal in both 2015 and 2025, then the first 302 species are accounted for (held as a "constant" in every year). Anything over 302 would be put in the vagrant category. Even if Noah saw all 302 annual birds back in 2015, that leaves only 34 remaining of the 336 to be the bonus vagrant birds. In 2015, Noah reported 86.6% of the confirmed species. This was not enough for a new annual state record. However, in 2017 the total confirmed bird species count was up to 348. A new annual state record was set with 316 species reported by the top eBirder, or 90.8%. The point here is that a lower vagrant year similar to 2015 can impede setting new records, but those are the breaks. In addition, remember from our formula in Figure 6, that vagrants are only one piece of the puzzle for maximizing the number of species recorded. We knew going into 2025 that in addition to the 302 annual birds, we needed a year with several dozen vagrants if we were going to break the 322 record set in 2021. Going back to our goals, we had set our mission to see over 300 species. Birders reporting annual species counts exceeding 300 in Maine is impressive, Big Year or not. In 2025, there were two other birders besides us who exceeded 300 species in Maine. The gap between us and the next closest eBirder was 23 species. It is here where we believe our process and strategy set us apart from the rest of the pack - further validation. Our process was efficient. We hit 300 species on September 18. At that point, we knew there was only one path for us to take - raise the bar and set a new record.

This brings us to the next point. What if back in 2015 there were just as many vagrants as in 2025? Maybe there *were* just as many vagrants back then. Huh? Consider that concept for a moment. eBird existed in 2015, but there were fewer users. The chat groups existed, but they were in a different forum and a bit more cumbersome. The COVID pandemic had not happened yet, so there were also presumably fewer birders. Collectively, all of this *could* indicate that the vagrants were always there, but no one found them. The early technology and spottier communication coupled with the sparsity of birders years ago may have left a number of vagrants undetected. Who knows?

The communication piece cannot be underestimated. We mentioned past technology. How did one share sighting information and pass the berry in a timely manner when the technology was cumbersome? Today, advances in technology, including social media, may contribute to the berry passing in a big way. Remember the old saying, you must give in order to receive? The upside from passing the berry will be less impressive if one chooses to hold sightings too close and with less sharing. In our Big Year, we could actually *feel* the momentum that was being created by passing the berry. Sharing information had a slow return at first. But then, the passing back to us started to snowball. Therefore, if the technology and communication tools are either not used or hampered in any way, the berry passing may stall, at best. In our opinion, it is possible that in a lower vagrant year like 2015, the vagrants may have existed, but the technology and sharing capability may have been in a different evolutionary place.

Finally, we mentioned in The Experiment chapter that we decided to disclose our goal of 300 to other birders. In hindsight, that was a good choice and an important one. From that perspective, the berry passing started on day one. The public disclosure, however, did have at least one downside. Other birders and friends would often ask where we were going the next day or next week. The fact is, we did not devise our specific plan until the evening before. Sometimes, we would have a plan the evening before and then it would change once we met at the park-n-ride. That was fine. It worked. Our process was living and flexible. Our strategy was specific, but not a script. When other birders wanted to know where we were going next, we simply didn't know.

Our eBird checklists, made public and promptly posted, were our best and most timely offering to the birding community.

Going back to the formula where this chapter started, we have reflected quite a bit about "weighting" the factors. Not all factors of the formula are equal contributors. We can share how our weighting unfolded now that we have the data and Big Year experience. Refer to Figure 8. The combination of team and process, in our specific Big Year, is a single unit, and weighted together. Team without our process and vice versa, makes no sense. The Integrated Birding *is* The Experiment. Collaboration and our strategic process were, by far, the primary contributors to our success. With that in mind, we weight the Team/Process portion at 75%. We estimate the Sharing portion to be weighted at 15%. Passing the berry provided even more positive return than we anticipated, and more than relying on an unknowable vagrant year. That leaves 10% weight for the Vagrant portion. It's true that a lower vagrant year could make it improbable to set new records, but an impressive birding year is still possible. Vagrants are also not in our control. Therefore, rely on other birders to help find the vagrants and pass you a berry in reciprocation for all the berries that you have passed them. Simple. Right?!!!

Figure 8. Weighted Formula

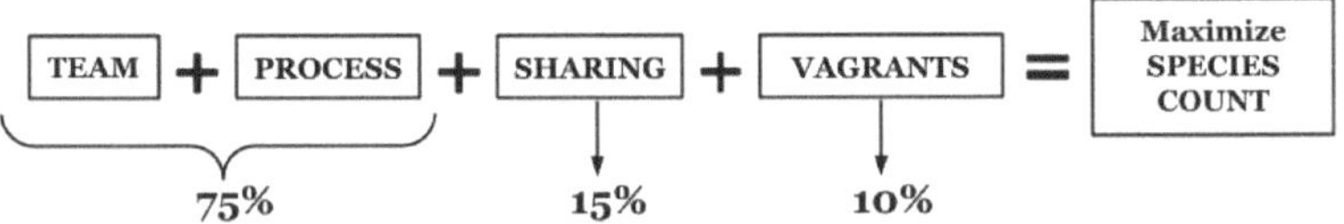

What is possible when two bird-loving people come together, form a team, and apply both their overlapping and unique skills to see the most bird species in Maine in one year? The answer:

- The bar is raised and new records are set.
    - Teamwork was the main theme of The Experiment. With a two-person team, we were able to magnify the reach of our Big Year.
    - eBird checklists using best practice documentation was vital to high quality output, thereby demonstrating a high bar.
    - Communication with the birding community through text, chat groups, and social media allowed for transparency and credibility. When all is combined, the potential is created for new records to be set.

- Communities are strengthened.
    - Many in the birding community watched our Big Year progress. At the onset, we openly shared our Big Year mission of observing 300+ bird species in Maine. Birders and non-birders alike enjoyed following our project and became valuable extended team members.

- Life lessons are solidified.
    - Despite our drive to find new species, we often paused to take in the scenery, wildlife, and flora. Making time to reset priorities and knowing what is important became essential for our positive mindset. It's not always just about the birds.
    - The bird population can reflect the spectrum and character of the human population. For example, some birds know that in order to receive, they must pass the berry. As humans, we too, receive joy when we give. Sharing rare bird information with our fellow birders became our berry. We passed the berry often, and in return the berry was passed back to us.

Now, go do birding!

REFERENCES

1. Maine Bird Records Committee. google.com/site/mainebirdrecordscommittee, Review List, late 2024.
2. Kaufman, Kenn. *Kingbird Highway: The Biggest Year in the Life of an Extreme Birder*. Houghton Mifflin Harcourt, pp.196-197, 2006.
3. Skrentny, Jeff. *"What Counts? And Why? Says Who?"* Winging It, Newsletter of the American Birding Association, vol. 24, no. 6, Dec 2012.
4. Lund, Nick. "Is This Bird ABA Countable?" The Birdist.com, June 16, 2013.
5. Hitchcox, Doug. "A Growing Trend." Maine Audubon Habitat, Spring 2025.
6. Maine Audubon Staff. "Red-bellied Woodpeckers on the Rise in Maine." Maine Audubon.org. January 20, 2015.
7. Christmas Bird Count Tracking Tool. "Where Have All The Birds Gone?" Audubon.org/community-science/christmas-bird-count.

Date: 2025

Project: An Experiment In Birding: Acknowledgements

Continued from Page: 90

There are so many people to Thank. The support we received through the course of our Big Year was extensive. We ask for forgiveness in the event we inadvertantly omitted someone.

Part A. Special thank you to Derek L., John L., Bill T., and Alex L. for regularly and promptly reaching out with intel. You are all honorary members of our 2025 Big Year team.

Part B. There were a number of folks who welcomed us to their private property so that we could enjoy some rare finds. These were special moments for us - such a pleasure to meet you and share the joy of birding. Grateful to: Bill + Carol, Patty, Jodi, Cathy + John, Brendan T., Brendan M, Lisa, Peter + Jennifer, Sue + Bill, MaryAnne, Donna, Brit + Rob, Don + Merrie, Carolynn + Dave, Carla + Gregory, The Cole's, Frank

Part C. The list of our birding friends who each had their own role to play in our Big Year is substantial. Gratitude to: Bill S., Bird, Bill + Monica, Bob D., Bob K., Brad, Brit, Cecile, Charles + Laura, Dan, David A., David N., Dee + Ed, Delia, Donna, Doug, Ed H., Ethan + Ingrid, Evan, Gordon, Karina + Mark, Jeanette, Jeff, Jose, Josh, Julie, Kevin, Kristen, Lauren, Linda + Turk, Leon, Lewis (special thanks for 2 rescues; once from the mudflats, once from a sinkhole), Louis, Lucienne, Luke, Mackenzie, Mael, Magill, Marian, Mark, Matt, Michael, Nick, Pam, Pete, Rich M., Richard, Rob, Rob + Tracy, Ruby + Trevor, Sally, Tim, Tom, Tora, Walter, Will B., Will S., Zach, Maine Audubon Staff.

Part D. There are tons of non-birding people to acknowledge. Thank you for cheering us on: Alex W., Roberta (your review of the book manuscript was so appreciated), our life friends, our social media friends, Fire + Ice, the Noah's Birding Tours family, Noah's work crew, Brad + Stacey and their daughters Eden, Cora, and Wren.

Part E. Our families were truly tested during 2025. We have immeasurable love and gratitude to Emma (Stacey's extraordinary daughter), Becky (Noah's amazing wife), Tyler (Noah's awesome son), Steve, Chris, Noah's mom and dad, Ian, Erica, Kelly, Trixie and Teddy.

Part F. We would also like to thank each other. Our Big Year may have come to an end, but our friendship has just begun.

Date:	Approved by:	Continued on Page:
2026	[signatures]	The End

Photo courtesy of Walter Brooks

N: Do you think we can do a Little Year next year?

S: Yes, please.

ABOUT THE AUTHORS

Stacey Pazar Huth, PhD, was raised on Tanager Street in Arlington, Massachusetts, and has made Southern Maine her home for the past 35 years. She holds a doctorate in chemistry, and spent more than 30 years as a corporate leader and scientist. She led teams in the research and development of diagnostic products in both the human health and veterinary markets. Amongst her proudest professional contributions was leading a technical team at Abbott Laboratories for the development of the BinaxNOW COVID-19 Antigen Card. After retiring from corporate life, she founded Tanager Street, LLC, a scientific consulting firm. Stacey is an active member and Trustee of the Maine Audubon Society and the proud mother of her adult daughter, Emma. Now an empty nester, she has returned to her lifelong love of birds and enjoys exploring Maine with her birding friends.

ABOUT THE AUTHORS

Noah Gibb has been a Mainer all his life. He always loved watching birds in his backyard as a boy. In his mid twenties, his older brother gave him a digital camera. It was then that he became obsessed with birds, birding, and bird photography. Noah has earned a solid birding reputation in Maine's birding community for his keen visual and auditory bird identification skills, calm demeanor, and sense of humor. In addition to his full-time job, he owns and operates a birding tour business, Noah's Birding Tours, LLC. Noah is impressive to watch at Maine beaches during shorebird season when he singles out a Western Sandpiper amongst the vast numbers of other similar shorebirds. A Maine Audubon volunteer since 2013, Noah leads weekly Scarborough Marsh bird walks during the summer months. In addition to a long list of other volunteer activities, he also created an internal digital channel to help build the birding community at his place of employment. Noah lives in Southern Maine with his lovely wife and their son.

If you would like to reach out to the authors, please contact them at AnExpInBirding@gmail.com or follow on social media.

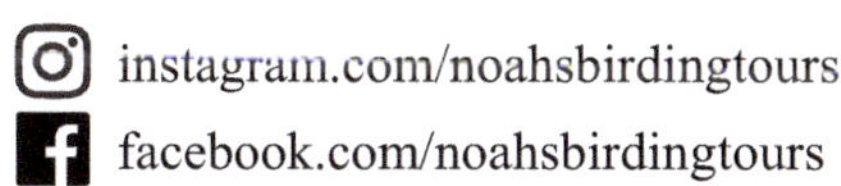

Caspian Tern

www.ingramcontent.com/pod-product-compliance
Lightning Source LLC
LaVergne TN
LVHW052255100826
845147LV00001B/47

* 9 7 9 8 9 9 4 7 0 1 8 0 5 *